CHRIS VOSS

Beacons of Leadership: Inspiring Lessons of Success in Business and Innovation

First published by Christian Voss 2021

First edition

ISBN: 978-1-08-792098-6

This book was professionally typeset on Reedsy.
Find out more at reedsy.com

Dedicated to my Mom.
Thank you for all the love and support

Contents

IV   Part Four

Preface

Welcome to my 35 years of experiences and lessons as the CEO of my own companies since I was 18 years of age. What if you could access all the gold nuggets of my "CEO Toolbox" that I've accrued over my vast career? You could pay me as a coach to consult with you and/or your company, or you could have admittance to some of it within this book.

My experience that I will share with you comes from being a CEO, owning interests in companies in the realm of mortgages, real estate, stock markets, mall retailing, computer sales, clothing lines, talent agencies, courier companies, personnel companies, call centers, construction, pay per call industry, club promotions, podcasting, speaking, and social media, etc.

As you can imagine from that list of industries, there are a multitude of insights from my experiences in leadership, management, startup and life that I'll be sharing with you. I'll give you the rich details of my CEO/Entrepreneurs Toolbox I used to scale business success, innovate and build companies.

I'll peel back the curtain on the vision, lessons and hard work that I put in to build successful multi-million dollar brick and mortar companies from a few thousand dollars. I will also share the techniques I used to innovate and run them so well I ran competitors into bankruptcy.

I'll tell you how I saved companies from partner sabotage and pulled companies back from the brink of bankruptcy. I share with you how many times I reinvented myself and business to recover from the 2008 recession and other times my life or business was disrupted and how I survived and rebuilt.

I'll share how I became successful in social media launching the original award-winning Forbes Top 50 Brand in 2008, The Chris Voss Show, to become a leader over a nearly 400,000 followers and give back to people my experience and know-how along with building The Chris Voss Show Podcast.

But Who is Chris Voss?

I've been a serial entrepreneur since the age of 18, but as you'll read, I was in sales and running a business as a kid. I have been a CEO of all my nearly 30 companies, building and managing a multitude of corporations in different fields of the industry, that I've either outright owned or invested in.

At 53, it's been quite a ride, and I've learned so much that I've compiled and shared in this book, hoping you will learn from my success and failures. So my story of learning to innovate, sell and take entrepreneurial initiative started as a kid.

Many of you know me from my social media fame. In 2008, I established the "Chris Voss" name and brand on social media, starting with getting on Twitter early on and building influence as a leader, being at one time in the top 1000 on Twitter. In 2009, I established The Chris Voss Show blog at TheChrisVossShow.com, along with my YouTube channel under Chris Voss, sharing my business and life experiences.

I also launched The Chris Voss Show Podcast and started doing podcasts as well. To date, I own all the @ChrisVoss profiles across social media and URLs with the exception of the .com of my name, but I own ChrisVoss.net.

The Chris Voss Show has produced nearly 4200 posts, 4000+ YouTube videos, with almost 25 million video views and an endless amount of social media content, marketing and consulting. The Chris Voss Show Podcast is closing in on about 1000 podcasts and it's been a wild ride.

Since becoming a recognized name as a leader in social media, I've won many awards over the years, but here are some that stand out:

Forbes Top 50 Social Media Influencer, Consultant, Speaker, etc. The Chris Voss Show has almost 300,000+ followers.

- Top 100 Marketing Influencers

- Brand24 Top 100 Influencers
- Webinale: TOP 20 Influencer
- Top 15 Influencer of CES Show By DigiObs
- Top 50 Most Retweeted by Digital Marketers
- Top 30 Most Engaging Marketing Influencers
- My YouTube Channel has nearly 25 million views

Like many people, I had to fight in order to survive the late 2008 financial crises that destroyed my empire of companies, and I had to restart completely from scratch and tap into the inner origins of my CEO Toolbox and character to rise from the ashes of loss.

I'll share how I made them massively profitable, how you can be a leader in whatever stage you are at in your life, regardless of whatever position.

I based this book on my memories at age 53 as best as I can recall.

This is the journey of how it all began for me with many lessons you can use that I hope will change your life.

Look for additional book content, autographs, and other bonus content at BeaconsOfLeadership.com

Follow The Chris Voss Show Podcast at TheChrisVossShow.com

Acknowledgement

No man is an island. Life and projects like this represented an orchestra of sharing each other's audiences that helped inspire me to put my stories to paper. I am blessed to have the support and care of so many people I get to call friends and family. I thank you all.

The journey for this book began in early January 2021 when, out of the graciousness of his heart, Stephen A Pieraldi sent this "die hard" Android phone user a spare iPhone. I used the phone to launch my brand on a hot new app called Clubhouse.

At Clubhouse, I found a place to share and reminisce about many of the stories in this book. People loved them.....resulting in an impressive network of new friends. It made me realize people really loved my stories and they should finally go into a book. It was an interesting time to write a book in the depths of the COVID pandemic. Stephen set in motion the impetus for this. Many thanks Stephen.

Somewhere amid all of us talking about what to do after the COVID lock down as we all would emerge back into the world. I had talked about writing a book again and mentioned how many of my author friends committed to writing an hour a day in an accountability challenge group.

Blanca Cobb organized a group of us to accept the same challenge. While it was a mix of helping each other through writing at least an hour a day, it became apparent that I had gotten serious about writing my book. I realized I wasn't competing with the others in the group anymore.....I was competing with myself to get it done. If Blanca had not rounded us up to commit to do the daily writing challenge, I know I would have kept putting it off and this book would not be written today. Thanks for her help.

Rachel Whittaker also deserves a **VERY SPECIAL THANKS**. She was my

ONLY friend who, very early on, **read through the entire book**. I was barraged with conflicting advisors regarding the content and structure of the book. At a critical juncture of being stuck with pressure me to ditch the personal memoir stories, her read and feedback helped me believe in my stories I wanted to tell. I do not know where this book would be without it.

Another **very special** thanks to multi-book author Jude A. Morrow who saved me a ton of money and sanity in my book production costs. Also, thanks to Jonathan Green for his expert advice on publishing the book.

Thanks for all the support given by my Clubhouse, COVID, "foxhole" group. Especially for putting up with a crazy madman who wrote a book while on an intermittent fasting diet. As the saying goes, "Forgive me for what I might have said when I was starving", getting cabin fever from locking myself down for long writing spells while experiencing diet low blood sugar, losing over 60 pounds and counting.

At one point I was posting like Jack Nicholson in The Shining, "all work and no play..." My friends were likely taking votes on having me committed. The COVID lockdown was madness, and foxholes make interesting friends of necessity. I'm glad we made it out. I'll never forget the experience of it and all the friends I gained. Thanks for listening to all my madness to flush out the stories from my dusty memory.

For my mom, a retired educator, whose patient feedback and listening ear was much appreciated and very instrumental in putting the book together for print.

Thanks to the people who tried to destroy me financially over the years, giving me the marvelous stories & lessons for this book. Without your failed attempts, which allowed me to me triumph, I would not have the rich palette from which to paint my narrative. I learned so much, examples of which will help others across book sales and speaking stages. I hope you learned to be better.

Finally, to everyone who stood by my side, lifted me up, cheered me on with their encouragement, advice and insight, thank you sincerely.

Acknowledgment Page Sponsors: Neal Rapoport for being an excep-

tional best friend, brilliant marketer, YouTube reviewer, and so much more. Check out his website at www.rapoport.net

I

Part One

Beacons of Leadership Foundation

1

Beacons of Leadership

"If your actions inspire others to dream more, learn more, do more and become more, you are a leader."-John Quincy Adams

Inside this book, I've set forth the concept of what I call the "Beacons of Leadership." On the cover is an image of a lighthouse. The reason I chose a Lighthouse is that for centuries it has stood as a symbol of strength and safety. Built on lofty peaks, they were constructed to withstand the most powerful winds and storms. Their beacon of light gave hope and guidance to passing ships.

What I want to impart to you as a reader is that a leader is much like a lighthouse. We'll talk about how to think of yourself as a "leadership lighthouse" to your organization, your audience, your group, even your family.

Everyone around you can see your light on the peak and look to you for business guidance, inspiration, and motivation. Everyone is watching you, your employees, stockholders, partners, vendors, your board, people outside the company. You are a beacon broadcasting a lighted message to everyone who is looking towards you for guidance.

People follow leaders and are drawn to them. I think many of us need to realize that we can all be leaders and use our power to change the world. Being an excellent judge, being able to mold organizations, or a family environment and tone, comes down to the beacons you send forth in your personal leadership.

What is a "Leader"?

According to the Dictionary: "the action of leading a group of people or an organization." Others define an outstanding leader as someone who has integrity, ability to delegate, communicate, inspire people to do what they thought they couldn't. He/she has self-awareness, empathy, and influence.

So let's take a moment to define a "Leader" in your mind. How do you define leadership? How do others define leadership? Take a moment and write or think about some terms that come to mind for you about what leadership might be. Who are the leaders that you aspire to? Consider the traits you like in them. Write some down.

Now WHY do those leaders inspire you? This can give you some perspective on your own interests and assets as a leader. What are their talents that you aspire to have or wish you could develop? Again, sit down and make a list of what your leadership attributes are. Take a moment to consider it.

Being a leader, in my definition, means being a VISIONARY AND INSPIRING OTHER PEOPLE WITH PASSION. People like John F Kennedy, Steve Jobs, Elon Musk, Jeff Bezos and others. These are leaders who are brave enough to read the wind, the waves, the moon and stars and chart a course into the dark waters of the unknown. True leaders are smart and brave. True leaders are futurists.

Leadership Traits

In order for us to define top leadership traits that you can identify in yourself or possibly develop, we have to look at figuring them out and define them for a better understanding.

While the leadership principles I'll be describing here are kind of "blue sky" or "godlike" assuming you could master all of them, it's unlikely most leaders will encompass all of them, but let's get a sense of some of the top ones and how they can help each of us attain being a better leader that people will want to follow.

Here's a list of some attributes people have suggested to me:
Imparts vision
Inspiring and cloning other leaders
Calming presence, regulating energy
Motivates people to follow
Guidance
Lives their truth and inspires others
Position doesn't define leadership.
Captures the imaginations to inspire people to do better
Using weakness as strength

Position DOES NOT Define True Leadership.

I used to keep a sign on my desk that reminded me that my "Title" has to be "earned every day," and that just having the "title" doesn't make me a genuine leader.

Even though I was the CEO who owned 51% of my company, I knew that I still had to EARN people's respect as a leader. People would respect me as a "boss" out of obedience and fear, but I needed to be an inspiring leader. Over the years, I've seen so many managers who think that when they are given a title, that they automatically step into a role of leader that people will automatically respect and follow anywhere.

That's not the way it works. You have to EARN people's trust and respect to be a leader. You may think that you are the "Boss" but that doesn't mean you can motivate people to move mountains for you or march into battle with their hearts and minds fully behind you.

Are You An Inspiring Leader or Just A Manager?

Discussing this issue with some focus groups, the topic came up that not all CEO's, teachers, parents are truly influential leaders. They are more bosses or managers of people. A supervisor seems like a babysitter in its job description. To me, there are 2 types of people at top positions, inspiring leaders or just managers.

Not everyone is a person who can inspire and move people. Some can only be herders pushing people from behind, herding them from project to project. A leader pulls, a manager pushes.

It is important to recognize that there is a difference between being an inspiring leader rather than just being a manager. A manager is someone making sure all the boxes are checked and the basics are done. He performs his duties commanding people, whether he inspires them.

People do the work whether they respect the manager, sometimes out of fear, or sometimes doing the bare minimums. A manager pushes from the back, cracking the whip usually based on what they must do. Uninspired people do uninspired work. People follow managers because THEY HAVE TO.

The difference is a truly inspiring leader is someone people will follow because THEY WANT TO.

A true leader works from the front of his/her group, pointing off to the horizon for a far away lofty goal and inspiring their followers with passion to climb any mountain to get there. Leaders PULL everyone forward to that vision, enticement, and a better future.

People love to be inspired, to be motivated to feel a sense of something greater than themselves. They are filled with a leader's golden vision of a glorious future and destination that awaits and they work with that passionate fervor for the vision.

A leader is someone who is like the captain of a ship in a tossed frothy sea of a marketplace and trending winds. They look out across the horizon with no land in sight, calling upon their expertise and vision. A leader checks their compass, of their internal intuition. Then they tell the crew to chart their

6

course on a bearing that will lead them to a more vibrant future.

Part of being a leader is convincing his/her crew and the members aboard that a glistening shore lies out there in a land of bounty. Meanwhile, as a follower, you don't fully know how you will get there, but you trust the leader's exciting vision that evokes a passion in you and you are motivated to follow him or her almost anywhere.

Steve Jobs and other leaders were said to "suspend reality" or have a "reality distortion field" mentality. Where they can get their followers to follow them into ideas that seemed almost impossible, but the belief in the leader carries them through to breakthrough innovations.

The actual difference between a manager and leader is that a leader can conjure up people's own visions and imaginations and try to take them to places they have never been or seen before. Therefore, many times we celebrate those that lead us to places of great unknown. The "moonshot" type leaders are vaulted throughout all of history.

Ask yourself, how do the people who follow me see me? Do they see me as an inspiring, visionary, and passionate leader? Or just the boss?

Anyone Can Be A Leader

Anyone can be an inspiring leader whether it's the CEO, manager, front-line worker, parent, or everyday person just being nice to others. We all have the ability and opportunity to become leaders that can motivate people. Some of us can even become leaders in challenging or emergency moments where leaders are sometimes forged by the fire of being a hero.

Having the ability to be a leader is a developed skill. Also, being a leader is knowing your weaknesses and working to improve them to complete yourself as a whole leader. This is what I hope you learn from the book and will keep coming back to.

I wasn't the big communicator that I am today (probably too big a mouth now, my friends say sometimes), I was a quiet, introverted kid. I wasn't extroverted at all like I am now. I was one of those silent watchers in school, watching everyone having fun socializing and interacting.

I was an introvert and even thought people who were boisterous and full of ego and passion were jerks. But there is a healthy balance and you can learn to become an extrovert and an outgoing speaker and orator to motivate people and fire them up.

Around the country, there are the Dale Carnegie speaker training companies where many people have learned to overcome being shy and being more outgoing, even many of the successful speakers you may see on stage started out there.

The Challenge of Being a Leader

In addition, throughout this book, I'll share my thoughts on how I view leadership traits that helped me build my success. Being a CEO/Entrepreneur/Leader is one of the toughest jobs in the world and most of the toughest challenges you will face are in your mind.

It will challenge your paradigms and sometimes physically like nothing you might ever know. It will not only expand your mind, but the worry, the sleepless nights, the endless focus on business will stretch your boundaries and limits in ways you never thought possible.

On top of this, for those of you who want to be leaders in your own right, who want to recognize and expand your ability to be a leader, I've included tools to help you regardless of your place in life. In the following chapters, I'll walk you through some of my stories and lessons I learned, developed, and applied to become a leader in my life and business.

At the end of each chapter will be a roundup of the key traits of leadership I developed and used. At the end of the book, I'll summarize what is in my mind the top 5 leadership principles you should have or develop.

2

The 9 Dot Puzzle of Life

*"Imagination is more important than knowledge. Knowledge is limited.
Imagination encircles the world." - Albert Einstein.*

The 9 Dot Puzzle is the lesson that shaped the arc of my life, which I reference throughout the book.

In my early 20s, I'd taken a course taught by famed motivational speaker and trainer Lou Tice. It was a seminar that lasted over several days. One lesson in that course changed the entire trajectory of my life...his presentation of the "9 Dot Puzzle". You've probably heard or read about it, but I'd like to share with you the many ways it changed how I looked and approached thinking about innovation in business and life.

The lesson that Lou Tice taught helped me identify what I had been doing all my life at key moments. I'll be describing to you how it gave me a critical tool to put into my leadership toolbox that I would use all the time to innovate, grow, change my personal life and in business.

Since then, many writers have covered the 9 Dot Puzzle, but I used this paradigm to rethink everything in my life after that.

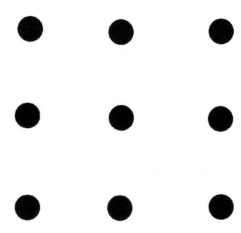

This is the Nine-Dot Puzzle. Draw this diagram on a piece of paper. Here is the challenge: You must connect ALL nine dots WITHOUT LIFTING the pen/pencil from the paper in 4 STRAIGHT lines once you begin. No curving allowed. All 4 lines must be 100% straight. Stop here until you can figure it out.

So how did you do? The solution is in the back of this book.

To complete the puzzle, you must extend 2 of the 4 straight lines OUTSIDE of the implied box to create a triangle or kite. Two of the lines have to extend outside of the box. Very few see it, because they have mentally made an invisible border they ASSUME they cannot cross. But there are no rules given in the instructions that govern that.

Most people think that you have to stay inside of the invisible box that is implied by the dots. But there is no box, just the formation of the 3x3 dots. The people who adopt this self limiting "box" theory limit their ability to complete the puzzle. In their mind, they are inside a box of their own making.

It is surprising when most people do the puzzle; they try to stay inside their mentally created self-limiting box that makes them unable to expand outside their own unimagined boundaries. The lesson is that we all do this with so many things in our lives. People invent their own limitations essentially. Just like they do in life and business.

We all create these self-limiting boxes that trap us in restrictive beliefs that imprison our true potential. Social norms, business norms, business processes, for example, when someone says, "Well, this is the way we've always done it, so I've never questioned why."

With self-limiting thinking, we build scotomas or blind spots that make it so we can't see out of the box. People accept so many per-constructed self limiting norms or beliefs. They have blind spots not being able to see what they don't know.

Many of them are social, economic or the attitude of "Well, that's just the way things are". They never challenge ideas or idioms around their business. Their mind traps them inside the box with their self limiting belief system.

The lesson is to learn to think "outside of the box." You must learn to see or imagine the endless possibilities of all the things outside of it. So when you hear that phrase I'll be using throughout the book, you'll know what I'm referring to. This was one of the key tools in my leadership toolbox.

Hopefully, you will use it to redefine your life and break out of your own boxes. You can use this tool to seek new innovations in your company and design more possibilities outside of the box that holds you back.

But first we need to look at my thinking up to that point and go back in time to where I developed into an innovative visionary leader...

II

Part Two

My Stories & Lessons of Building A Leader

3

Analog Kid

"Here's to the crazy ones. The misfits. The rebels. The troublemakers. The round pegs in the square holes. The ones who see things differently. They're not fond of rules. And they have no respect for the status quo. You can quote them, disagree with them, glorify or vilify them. About the only thing you can't do is ignore them. Because they change things. " -Rob Siltanen

The Dreamer & The Early Sales Lessons

The first experience I had with sales, rejection and courage, which would become the building blocks of my future leadership character, was selling Scout-O-Rama tickets as a boy scout. Scout-O-Rama was usually a once a year event where all the scouts come together…it was a bit like a carnival with lots of family fun.

Top prize was two tickets to a Los Angeles Dodgers game. I wanted so badly to win them. It was a tier "commission" award system where basically depending on how many tickets you sold, the better the award would be.

Growing up in Southern California, I was a Los Angeles Dodgers baseball fan, and my favorite player was Steve Garvey. Their manager, Tommy Lasorda, was a heck of a respected leader. I so wanted to go to a game and see my idols. My golden ticket was to sell enough to earn the level of Scout-O-Rama sales that would allow my dad and I to go to a game.

Selling the tickets was a hard sell in the 1970s after the recession. People weren't that supportive of children trying to sell fundraisers, and some people were sometimes downright mean in their rejection. I'll never forget trying to sell tickets everywhere, door to door, always hustling. It was tough. People were unfriendly, hard and mean.

Over time and constantly selling, knocking on doors up and down the block, I had finally gotten within sight of my goal. I had cleaned out all the friends, families, church, and everyone I knew. I faced the daunting realization that the last bulk of my sales would have to come from total strangers. GULP!

So in order to reach my goal, I had my parents drop me off at the local Ralph's Grocery Store in Southern California. I stood at the old style automatic doors with one door in, one door out at the center so I could catch people coming and going.

I was a 9-10-year-old kid looking up at these towering adults asking them for a moment of time to pitch them. Keep in mind, I was all alone. My parents had dropped me off, and it was just a little old me all by myself trying to sell to complete strangers. I was in the Cub Scouts and there I was there in my spiffy little uniform, trying to look as official and professional as one could at that age.

As people passed through the entrance and exit, I was sitting between the automatic doors as they opened and closed, trying to pitch to people as they walked in and out. I did it for hours and it was brutal. The whole time I struggled and fought back, wanting to quit from the rejection, but I made a solemn promise to myself that when I became an adult, I would never be mean to children who were trying to sell something.

That promise helped me strengthen my resolve to not quit that day. I'll never forget how hard it was to look up at adults towering over you and trying to sell something to them. It's so intimidating. Finally, though, I sold enough tickets to win that Dodgers game prize.

I had squeezed off enough sales to hit the goal and the Dodgers tickets award was mine. There it was, without me even realizing till later, my first sales job, first commission, first experiences with sales, rejection and perseverance to

16

build my character, along with a vision for how to be a better adult.

Now as an adult, I follow that promise to my younger self; I have a rule to help inspire kids who are out trying to sell, and I make it a point that if they pitch me, I will buy from them. Sometimes if they are selling girl scout cookies or school fundraisers, I'll just hand them $20 and tell them to keep the product to sell to someone else.

They just met their first luxury buyer, who tips. When their faces light up, I know there's a chance I possibly influenced a future CEO or leader.

When I do this, though, I have a hard and fast rule: THE CHILD HAS TO PITCH ME A SALES PITCH. Nothing complicated, it doesn't have to be a good pitch, they just have to experience putting it out there. The scariest part of asking for the sale is the potential for rejection or come what may. I have to see them stretch out and roll the dice.

I'll always stop, smile, listen intently and buy regardless of how bad the pitch is (these are kids not trained pros), sometimes telling them they did a great job and what they did right. If I think they can handle it, I'll give advice on a better pitch. It takes 5 minutes to build someone's character and change a life. It's that simple to be a beacon of influence as a leader to someone.

I'm not a fan of parents who take over the child's selling experience. I would discourage parents from ever doing that, instead build the children's character, don't carry them. Parents would come into my office to get everyone to buy for their children's projects. I would ask them to please bring them to me and have them pitch me.

Most times the parents won't and they do not know the loss not only in developing their child but the amount I'd gladly contribute.

I always support them when I can. It's easy to do and takes minutes, but IT IS EVERYTHING TO THESE DEVELOPING CHILDREN. Remember that the next time you are going into a store or some place where young people are pitching a fundraiser.

When you or I stop and take the time, we're building the future generation of potential leaders and character. You may support the next future leader or another Chris Voss.

Lessons From A Father

When we first moved to Utah from California, my father got into the stucco sub-contracting business. His company name was Superior Plastering Foundation & Stucco. He perfected the art of plastering foundations as Utah has deep basement walls that extend up above the ground level with ugly concrete seams and finish.

We'd "stucco" plaster cement onto the exposed foundations and finish it with a "float" to give the stucco a nice smooth finish.

As children, we'd spend our summers out on the job site with him, helping him with his work and keeping us out of our mother's hair. This was the age when mothers would toss you out of the house till dinner and you'd run around keeping yourself entertained building forts, tree houses, street football, anything until mom called you for dinner.

Life was about adventure and exploring. We learned much in building a zest for learning, discovery and being out in the world, which, sadly, most kids miss out on today.

Over that time, we learned to help our dad do the various details of the hard blue collar labor of stucco subcontracting. We learned to mix the cement for him, apply it to the foundation with trowels and then work to achieve a smooth finish. Depending on what he needed, we'd be trading out roles to support his day's work.

We helped our dad's assembly line process for the job, mixing the cement, carrying water and making sure he had help. After a time, I got good at the different activities and pretty much would work on one side of the house while he did another. We got to know all the tasks very well in a way which I never realized would, years later, change my life in the most unforeseen, extraordinary way.

The exciting part of the day was those lunch break trips to the 7-11 where we would get treated sometimes with an orange crush or sprite (no caffeine) and usually a lunch packed by our mom, which often comprised sandwiches, some fruit...nothing fancy.

I remember the tuna sandwiches...they were the worst. By the time we got around to eating them, after they had been in the cooler all day, it soaked the bread through and was soggy. One lesson here: toast your tuna bread to prevent that.

I guess you could say in a comedic way; I carry the scars of that experience to date. But you learn a lot of grit when you work hard and have to eat what's given at hand. Learn to be grateful for what you have, but it also makes you dream of a vision of someday wanting something more so you can have something better in the future.

It was hard work, interesting and sometimes fun. If dad was ignoring you, we could wander around and adventure in areas around a construction site or other houses being built. Many times I'd accidentally step on nails that would nearly impale your foot on a work site, and somehow I lived with the help of enough tetanus shots. Lots of sunburns and the rare heat stroke.

I did that many times; it built character, perseverance, and a hard work ethic. If I recall, eventually at one point my dad would pay us. I think it was 75 cents an hour, or a couple of bucks a day, and we could make a little money doing it.

I never knew how important learning all of this would become. As with many things we learn in life, we never know how many things will come in handy in the future.

Early Lessons In Business & Collections

My dad was quite the fellow. He was trying to take care of a household, which included four children, one of which was severely handicapped without having finished his college degree.

We had come back to Utah to get the support of relatives so that both my parents could finish their college degrees, but the construction work was all-consuming and he never got the time to go back. But working with him in his construction business, there were many business lessons to learn.

I would be with him when he would go to collect checks for his work from usually salty, short-tempered, bearish type contractors with no interest usually in being nice or sometimes paying people on projects that had become money losers at no fault of my fathers.

I witnessed many times contractors dodging my father at their offices for payment and the secretary always brushing him off. The hardest time was watching a contractor tell my dad the project was in bankruptcy or close to it and if he wanted to get paid, he would have to accept a pittance of what they owed, usually offering 50%, 25% or sometimes pennies on the dollar.

It was heartbreaking because usually the delivery was cold, rude, and hard. Take or leave it. Something or nothing.

Imagine standing there as a father with your children and being mistreated in that manner. My father had broad shoulders and a muscular frame from all the hard work. He was also short-tempered, but in the face of this he would keep his cool and negotiate.

This was in an age where it was mostly handshakes and no contracts. I learned many lessons watching these interactions and about collections being an important part of a business.

I learned what bankruptcy was and how businesses would use it to renegotiate debt. Dad would explain what the contractor meant when they said that we could try to get our money in courts and that the likelihood was nil.

I learned that sometimes business can take a loss and be unfair. But this was a part of being in business. Some people don't pay their debts.

My dad had some innovations as well. When a contractor was avoiding him so as not to pay, he had a unique way to get the money that is quite funny to look back on.

In the 80s, it was still an era where most of the women were homemakers and would be home during the day. My dad, in his work clothes, covered in dried cement bits that would never wash out.

His work pickup truck carried a cement mixer and all the elements of the cement that had sprayed out and over time covered the bed of the pickup truck. Traveling around we looked like a dusty, cement covered lot, but that was the work outfit. No use ruining new clothes, just wear the old cement covered ones.

So my father would find the address of the contractor's house that was dodging him for payment. At midday, we would park in front of the house and my father, with his sons in tow, would go to the door and ask for the contractor.

The wife would answer the door and he would explain he was there to get paid by the contractor and was usually told he wasn't at home.

My father would explain he'd been trying to get paid several times at the office, being dodged every time. He would politely tell the wife that we would sit out front in our ugly cement truck waiting until the man arrived home to pay him.

He would make a point of turning and pointing to the truck so that she would know exactly which one it was. So there we would park in front of the house, trying to keep occupied and listening to the radio.

Over the next while, you would see the wife constantly peeking through the curtains and on the phone. This was in a day before cell phones and the wives would worry that there was some stranger sitting out front with an ugly cement truck making the neighborhood look bad. In its simpleness, it was brilliant.

Usually, after a time the wife would come out to us to tell us she had chewed out her husband and we could go to the office to pick up a waiting check or sometimes the contractor themselves would come by and unhappily pay us on the spot.

It's now funny to look back...we must have tested a few marriages. But we got paid and collected our revenue. Another business lesson, perseverance and innovation, wins the day.

The BMX Bike - Learning Long Term Vision

Since about 10 years of age, I'd had a vision to build a $400 BMX bike and be a professional BMX racer. In California it was the trending rage and I wanted it so badly. I had grown up riding bikes all my life.

I had the "chopper bike" early on with the tall seat tail and would tape poker cards onto the frame so the wheel spokes would make a chopper sound.

It was that age of the 70s and 80s. You stayed outdoors till mom called you in. Life was an adventure around the neighborhoods and getting about required a bicycle to wander for miles, preferably a cool one, to make your friends envious.

I had seen the BMX bikes and freestyle take over the old skateboard pool grounds and was hooked. I got all the BMX magazines and ripped out all pages of the parts I wanted to build my $400 dream bike vision.

My family wasn't rich, and I'd have to earn nearly everything. It was a multi-year vision I embarked on and my first lessons on building a dream, nurturing it and working hard to make it happen.

This character building helped me later when I started my own companies or in anything I wanted to build that took time...you have to stay goal focused and build it.

So the vision was that over 2-3 years I would save up my money, buy a part here and there and assemble it. It was hard because I would just get a piece here, a piece there and for most of those years I was looking at this unassembled mass of parts just waiting for them to be complete so I could ride all the ramps and tracks I imagined and dreamed in my head.

I remember having just the frame first, a big step in the goal process. For our birthday & holiday gifts, my parents allotted me and my siblings a max $50 "gift ask" and with extra relative hustling, I'd gain rims, handlebars, and other expensive high-quality parts for my future BMX racing career.

It took me those 2-3 years to build a really great bike and lots of the work, but I was always doing it, working to the achievement of my vision.

To gain the parts, I looked for any job to pick up money. The vision drove me to get that bike built and achieve my dreams. Much of the work was hustle selling, clients and early entrepreneur stuff that actually began when I was around 9-10 years old when I learned what working and a job was.

Weirdly, I really didn't understand that what I was doing was entrepreneurial. I was just a kid with a vision and a burning desire.

Technically, my first self employment business was mowing lawns and hustling for business. Early on, I learned I could knock on neighbors' doors and sell them to mow their lawns for money. It was $5 for the front yard and $5 for the back.

And it was hot out in the sun, but it taught me about work ethic, serving and building clients, along with the rewards of having money.

Sometimes you'd be halfway done mowing and want to quit, but you had to force yourself to follow through with the commitment you had made to your client. It was early client management and customer service. Although $5 doesn't seem like a lot, in the 80s it was. A candy bar was still 25 cents. But it really shaped me.

Hard work and fighting through jobs and then building a clientele where you could have repeat business was paramount. Being a little kid banging on doors to sell adults, mowing and then collecting was rewarding in the end. It taught me I could have some control over my income and life.

Usually you'd have to knock on doors to sell or interact with your customer and collect the payments. The best part was getting the payment and feeling the reward and accomplishment. Then you learn if one house does this, lets go get more and build a list of regular weekly clients and that's what I did.

Sometimes I'd hire my brother or friend and pay them a cut as we doubled up work. I didn't realize what it meant, but someone should have taught me its value and importance to being a future entrepreneur. Parents should work to instill more of this.

Slinging Paper

At one point, I actually knocked on doors for "Grit Magazine", a bi-monthly magazine distributed throughout the United States. Grit magazine ran business opportunities in the classified section of other magazines alongside the "sea monkey" ads and the "X-Ray See Through Glasses".

I would have to do door-to-door sales in order to sell the magazines which involved collecting money and then handing the person their magazine.

It was a tough sell, and I experienced massive amounts of rejection. Unfortunately, I had to pay for all the magazines up front, and hoped I could sell them to get my money back. I really learned what a business model was and hated theirs. They really needed a better subscription model and I quit shortly after.

My first real "job" working for a real employer was when I was about 11 years old delivering newspapers. The company would deliver a stack of newspapers to my house. They needed to be folded along with a stack of advertising inserts, which, if I recall, was the bonus juice where you would get paid 25 cents per flier. But the kicker was you had to do all the ad flier inserting in the middle of the paper, folding and rubber-banding for delivery.

I developed an assembly line process which involved inserting the ad fliers, folding the newspaper, putting a rubber band around it and then tossing it into a pile, resulting in ink blackened hands as I sat in front of the TV.

Lots of breaking rubber bands to slap painfully at your hands through the process. But pain builds character, and we lived on. Then it was off to deliver them on my bike.

It was hard work balancing a massive stuffed bag on the front handlebars of my bike, especially during Utah Winters and hot summers.

Sliding a bicycle around in the snow was prone to errors, crashes, flat tires, skinned knees and all the challenges that come with that experience. I often got into many bike crashes as the paper bag would sometimes swing into the front tire spokes, upending me and the bike forward. Lots of scars and bruises, but definitely a character builder.

From time to time, I'd have to knock on doors and ask people to sign up for newspaper drives or specials the company would offer. I got to know people on my route, and they would sometimes wave. I took pride in my work. This was MY route. My territory. I ran it; it was mine.

Work Ethics

A lesson that made me think more about developing a strong work ethic and sense of commitment happened after two years of delivering newspapers. A person I knew closely joined the same company and worked in an adjacent paper route territory next to mine.

He had been working at it for nearly 6 months, and we would help each other fold and insert the ads for our routes.

Then one day someone caught him dumping his bag of hundreds of papers into a local gas station's dumpster. He thought he had figured out a way to cheat the system, skip the work, and still get paid in an unsupervised position. Turns out he'd been doing that for some time and they fired him.

It had never crossed my mind to be dishonest and cheat my employer. I took pride in my work and territory, and that meant something to me. It was a very important lesson to make me understand and value my commitment to my work values.

My First Leadership & Coaching Lesson

The newspaper that I worked for threw a party for all the employees. I remember the Utah Jazz coach Frank Layden coming to the party. He talked to us about leadership and other things.

One thing that stuck with me for all my career I'd reflect on was how he described that as a coach surrounded by multi-million dollar athletes, he still had to lead them and motivate them. That really blew my mind.

He said, most people ASSUME that since these players make all this money, they don't need leadership, management or motivation...it was completely the opposite. Even though the players were at the top of their game, they still needed a coach, a guide, a leader to give them a vision and help them improve to be better. Many times, he had to kick them up a notch in motivation. I never forgot that story and what it meant.

Becoming a Leader

In Utah, you couldn't start working until you were 16 years old, but at 14 I could accept a job as long as it was not out in the public eye. So I started working at a locally owned grocery store on the night shift as a "shelf stocker." I think I started at $2.85 an hour, but you could eventually get up to $3.35 with hard work, time, and promotions. It was fun, and I learned a lot.

In fact, it really was the first time I'd held a job where you worked with other people daily. The camaraderie was fun, and I did that for a couple of years. I took pride in my work, and over time I advanced, eventually getting to be the head stocker over all the stock crew.

I was the boss, a leader, and I had to not only give directions to the crew, but keep schedules and workers motivated and happy, which was both challenging and rewarding. Many times I worked in the store during public hours, opening the front door, helping with last-minute shelf stocking, moving palettes and unloading trucks.

This was where I started learning to be a leader and have that awareness, insight and responsibility to take care of "my store," especially in the middle of the night as we stocked and were all alone.

Upon reaching age 16, I could now move to the front of the store as a grocery bagger. This allowed me to work during the day. I went from being a stocking manager to starting over as a lowly bagger and now had to work my way back up again. The boss was a gruff and angry old man who didn't like me very much after I interrupted him once during his tendency to hit on cute young cashiers.

He resented me from that day forward and, though I hoped he would promote me, he passed me over a few times in spite. Finally, my strong work ethic paid off, and he made me the Assistant Head Bagger.

As one of two Assistant Head Baggers, he still kept passing me over for further promotion. Instead, he promoted those who were recently hired. After a while, I quit caring about trying to win his approval and realized I should just work hard for myself, my pride and work ethic. I didn't care whether he promoted me and just enjoyed mastering my work and being efficient.

Due diligence paid off…he finally had to recognize me as one of his top workers, and I became the Head Bagger, which meant overseeing the bagging team. There was much more responsibility, which included schedule making and knowing when to send employees home early, depending on how busy the store was.

After seeing my leadership excel, my boss finally treated me better, liked me, and trusted me with the position. Once again, I had the keys to the store and would open up in the mornings and close it on night shifts. This was MY store. I had persevered, done the hard work in the face of massive resistance, and won the battle. I was proud of it...I'd worked hard.

There were more duties, such as interviewing and hiring people. I'd have to train them on the job. I learned more about how to motivate, lead, and sometimes have to let people go. It taught me so much work ethic, customer service, pride and value in MY store.

After almost two years, I left the store and moved on to better pay. I worked at Pizza Hut and McDonald's at the same time till I was about 18 and this is how my career at being a CEO of my own companies began.

In each of our lives, there are things we learn that shape us, that build the character of a leader. At an early age, I was shaping the skill of having a strong work ethic. But there were more lessons to come...

Leadership Lessons:

- Vision
- Attitude
- Courage
- Perseverance
- Self-Reliance
- Handling Rejection
- Overcoming Adversity
- Learning to Sell & Service Customers
- Business Modeling
- Business Collections & Bankruptcy

4

A Young Innovator

"The nonchalance of boys who are sure of a dinner, and would disdain as much as a lord to do or say aught to conciliate one, is the healthy attitude of human nature"-Ralph Waldo Emerson

"Thank you for firing me for not cutting my hair," I said as I shook and held my ex-managers hand, looking him in the eyes, "You've changed my whole life for the better and now at 18, I make far more money than you in just a few months."

My first innovations of thinking "outside of the box" and constrictive social paradigms began in high school. It also was a way to design outside of norms and consider possibilities. You hear of many successful leaders who didn't fit in school, leaders who largely dropped out keeping the curricula that they like, such as Steve Jobs, Mark Zuckerberg and others that also didn't finish school.

Like them, some of my favorite teachers and classes flunked me because I didn't follow all the exams and reports, but because I focused more on the core content, learning and ignored the testing, I think I absorbed more than others.

I remember graduating with fellow high schoolers who still couldn't spell and had learned very little. Typewriting was the most important and valuable class I'd ever taken. Most of my school was largely financially worthless.

When I was twelve years old, my parents sold their home in California and moved back to Utah. The goal of both of my parents was to finish their college degrees. California schools were years ahead of Utah, so when I started school in Utah, I tested to be one or two grades ahead. Being ahead and bored, I quickly became disinterested in school and the format didn't fit my brain and process. I wasn't a bright student, and I hated the formalities of it.

I also missed California, the beach, the sun, and freedom. Even our school hallways were outdoors in California. Utah was awful with freezing temperatures, coats, and dark skies most of the year. I had gone from a beautiful sunny fun filled world to a dark, depressing environment.

Sadly, after arriving in Utah, my youngest sister, Annalisa, was born. What happened to her would change the whole trajectory of our family dynamic... because of the doctor's mistakes, she was left severely mentally and physically handicapped. My parents' dreams of furthering their own education had to be put on hold...my mother spent the next two years of "Annie's" life just trying to keep her alive and thriving.

Early on I suffered from the "CEO disease" being later diagnosed with ADHD & OCD. So many CEOs have some variation of it, that it's been widely termed the "CEO disease." It only grew worse when I hit high school.

I drove my teachers mad with my overactive bored brain, drumming on my desk and tapping the nerve in my foot that would cause my leg to bounce up and down endlessly.

I was always getting yelled at by my teachers. One day, my psychology teacher told me that my problem was an overactive brain that was bored and exhibited its activity in ways that disrupted the classroom.

Being in Utah, they have local religious seminaries right off the school's properties and religious parents would have their children take classes in it. At the start of my Junior school year, me and a friend acted out, disrupting the religious class, clearly resenting being there and I guess we got very out of hand and we were both sent to the Vice Principal's office.

Back in the Vice Principal's office, he read us the usual riot act. He called the seminary teacher to tell him we had agreed to be good, but I guess we had upset the seminary teacher so much we were told we were not welcome back, ever. Here it was, the start of my junior year, and all the classes were full and booked.

The Vice Principal was very frustrated with us and stated he'd have to figure out what to do with us and that the next day we should report to the front office and sit on the couch to pass the block class time of 1.5 hours until he could fix it.

So we did that. We sat on the couch talking while the office ladies watched us and after about 45 minutes, the Vice Principal wandered in. He took one look at us and started asking what we were doing there and why we weren't in class?

He had totally forgotten us, we soon profitably realized. We reminded him of his instructions, which he then remembered from the prior day he went off to do whatever it was Vice Principals do. This was my first memorable "out of the box" moment.

My friend and I talked with each other about whether he would ever remember us again. We came up with an ingenious plan. The next day we showed up again and then after a bit we both went off to the bathroom and then out to the driver's license training area to hide out. So the two of us tested our theory that he would forget about us and we were dead on.

We never went back and used the time to do what we wanted. Together, we were off the map of the high school agenda. He never noticed we were missing and totally forgot about us.

We had Block Class schedules of 90 minutes per class, so suddenly we had a ton of free time and it was next to our half an hour normal lunch, so now we had two hours for lunch! So we would walk daily about a mile down the road and eat lunch at Pizza Hut.

We'd relax, eat and then walk back sometimes to have lunch with our friends. It was quite fun. No one was the wiser. The Vice Principal never remembered us, even when he saw us in the hallways. We did that for the rest of the year unnoticed, actually signing up for seminary in the 2nd semester and never showing up.

More "Out of the Box" innovations

Book/Class formal learning wasn't my thing. My grades were poor, and it was obvious I wasn't going to Harvard or Yale. Because of my family's low income, I was eligible for Pell Grants to go to college.

My grades and lack of interest in formal education were bad…I would not get scholarships or anything as I was pushing out of the norms and breaking models, as you will see. I hated the rigid formality.

Then, in my senior year, I found out my friend was leaving school early because he had completed all the required credits. I found out how he did it. I was blown away. All this time I had been blindly accepting the school norms of their "box" and hadn't seen outside of it.

Turns out if I completed and passed all my classes, I would have completed 52 credits. Yet I discovered I only needed like 26 credits to graduate? What was this evil I had found? I was being forced to double the classwork I didn't have to do? Time for innovation. I had already flunked some classes and was a D to D- student.

So figuring all this process out, I mapped which classes I needed to pass to graduate and which were the filler ones. I started just mentally "checking out" in those classes by sleeping on the desk, disconnecting, and flunking. I'd tried to eek out a D- grade, but it caught up to me.

Early in making this change, one of my teachers took me aside and asked why I wasn't caring or doing anything in the class. I politely explained to her what I had figured out and what my innovative plan was.

She was horrified and aghast, followed by anger. NO ONE HAD EVER THOUGHT OF GOING OUTSIDE OF THE BOX THIS WAY OR THE APPROACH. I created something way off the map. I was nice. I just said I'd figured it all out and knew which classes I didn't need to graduate and intended to fail them.

She sternly told me then that she didn't want me to even bother attending her class, as she was offended that I wasn't willing to learn. The deal she insisted on would be that she would mark me as "present," but she didn't want me to show up. Out of the Box, total innovation in my teens.

Then I was smart enough to replicate that successful model to move it forward. I went to the other three classes I had determined I could flunk and told the teachers the deal my one teacher had struck with me. They did the same...I was not welcome in their class, didn't show up and they would mark me as attending.

I was a deal maker and free to do what I wanted for half a day each day. I could attend both block lunches and see all my friends at school. It was brilliant. I graduated high school with 26 of 26 credits that I needed to pass.

I want to say in hindsight that what I did was highly offensive to teachers who are caretakers to the cradle of educating our society with a love and passion for their students, while being horribly underpaid.

My mother finished her degree in elementary education and became an award-winning educator and a fearless advocate for programs for physically disabled children like my younger sister.

My older sister would also become a teacher, both dedicated to their professions and the children they taught. One vision my mother had was to see students placed in classroom settings that would address their dominant learning style and dealing with issues pertaining to the ADD/ADHD child.

The Road To Entrepreneur Fate

When I was 18, I was working at McDonald's. I was a Heavy Metal rocker, and I had very long hair and wore concert t-shirts all the time...which was frowned upon in the conservative community in which I lived.

I worked as a cook and loved it. I would entertain myself sometimes by quietly singing to myself, waving to people at the counter, or being funny. I'd trial and error sometimes the burgers with a little flair of additional ingredients, like an extra shot of special sauce on the Big Mac, and people would actually come compliment me as having the best McDonald's burgers they had ever had. This was again something I took pride in. It was MY grill as a cook. It was my job to do my best.

It was an early example of how I could tweak things and make customers happy. At the store, there was a revolving shift of 5 managers and all the managers liked me except for a single solitary one. This manager of McDonald's was ultra religious and didn't like my long hair and rocker fashion looks.

He felt it was satanic along with my heavy metal rock t-shirts and everything else about me, etc. So, he started bullying me.

Though I would ignore him, he would take delight in trying to antagonize me or set me off, but I would keep to my stoic self and carry on. He was just a low level manager with a wife and kids, likely miserable in a low-level job.

I always got the idea that he hated me because I was so free and open-minded. I probably represented some failure in his life. Even though I tried to ignore, sidestep and avoid him, he would beeline to pick on me when he saw me.

One way he finally got after me was my long rocker hair. He decided that I should have to cut my hair since I was a cook, and he didn't want hair in the food or that was his excuse. He kept bugging me about it and finally he instructed me that if I wanted to keep my job, I'd have to cut my hair or be fired... the ultimate threat.

I talked to the other managers, and they said it was up to him. I didn't know what to do. The big dilemma of being bullied at work: Cut your identity hair or lose your job. It, of course, seemed highly unfair.

Then I thought outside of the box to innovate again, questioning and polling reality. I thought, wait a minute, women working here have long hair too, and they wore hair nets that wound their hair up into their hats. I asked the women at the store how it worked and bought me a hair net.

So I started wearing a hair bun underneath my hat so that my long hair wouldn't show at work and my long hair wouldn't fall into the food.

I got away with it for almost two months. He didn't realize what I had innovated. He seemed quite impressed with himself that I had submitted to his bullying and had conformed to cutting my hair to suit his religion and, more so, of just being a total jerk.

Busted!

Then one day he caught me taking my hair net out. He realized that I'd been fooling him the entire time about getting a haircut. Well, he hit the roof! He had fallen for it even though I was operating within my ethical and moral rights. My response was that if women can do it, so can men, and it was unfair to discriminate against me.

He fired me on the spot and changed my life for the better forever. Sometimes we think the darkest moments are bottom, but they are really a portal we need to push through to something better. I hope that's one less you learn from this book.

I went home and told my dad. He said, What are you going to do now? Here I was 18 years old, just graduated from high school, trying to figure out what to do with my life.

Over the years of my childhood, as previously written in the book, my dad had worked as a subcontractor, plastering foundations and doing stucco work. I had helped him during the summer with all the various aspects of his construction stucco business. One day he said to me, well you know how to do the work. Why don't you just start doing my subcontractor business, you can use my old tools and everything.

He'd since abandoned the business years earlier. New contractors had come on the scene, but he still had the expensive tools and a builder supply account I could use to buy cement, lime and other materials on credit.

So it was up to me to go get a new client base and use my experience to start my first business at 18. So I started my first business I'd learned from a kid and took on my dad's old business name - Superior Plastering Foundation and Stucco.

I printed up my new first business cards and started trying to get new clients...it was difficult. I knew the work, but my father had always hustled the business and had clients. My dad had left the business, had no clients and everything had to be rebuilt back up. I wasn't a salesperson by any stretch of the imagination. Now, I was going out and meeting these big burly, salty, gruff, very short-tempered contractors asking them to give me their business.

They were pretty surprised to see this young 18-year-old whippersnapper coming in saying that he owned a subcontracting business and wanted their work. Worse, I had no references or other contracting work to lay claim to other than the experience of my childhood. Contractors were highly skeptical of my new little startup.

So time again to use feedback, adapt and innovate. After some trial and error, the way I would approach contractors who were skeptical of my youth and experience, I would offer them a guarantee that I could do the work and they would like it or they wouldn't have to pay me. "If you don't like the quality, don't pay me, it's free, no charge. What do you have to lose?"

With the raised eyebrows of usually greedy and opportunistic contractors I'd learned from my lessons as a kid with my father, I struck the right nerve with people who didn't enjoy paying subcontractors, anyway.

They bit the bait, and I knew all I needed was to get a few jobs down, do skilled work, and they would be hooked to keep using me for all their other houses. AND keep paying me. I got the deals. Everyone paid because they needed me for more work. Overnight, after being fired for my long hair, I was successful and had built a small business.

It wasn't the first time, as you'll read further, that I would put all my money on the line to earn business with an ironclad "free try me offer." I tried to present myself as professionally as possible and honed my pitching skills as I'd be trying to break into the mean contracting business world.

Long story short, at 18 I thought I'd hit the mother load and was rolling in dough. There I was going from $3-$4 an hour at McDonald's to earning $18,000 a year and being my boss. It was a hell of a drug and freedom.

The Payoff of Succeeding Enemies

After a few months of consistent life changing success, I went down to my old McDonald's and smugly shook the hand of the manager who fired me, as I looked him in the eye. It was everything I'd dreamed it would be.

I nicely explained my newfound success and thanked him for firing me and changing my life and money. I also pointed out that now I made more than him, so thank you. He was dumbfounded, stunned, and perplexed.

It was one of those significant moments of your life that you remember forever. Overcoming adversity, I changed my life forever. It was a choice moment. I wish I could meet him today and tell him how far I went building multi-million dollar companies while he probably stayed at McDonald's.

The Big City

I moved up to Salt Lake City to be closer to my work and to the University of Utah. Since my parents were low income and my grades were nowhere near going to get me a scholarship, the plan had always been to get a Pell grant to go to college. I chose the University of Utah.

In the meantime, I had this successful stucco business going, so I needed to make a choice of what to do. Soon I got the Pell Grant check and signed it over to the school. Then I arranged my classes, picked out everything needed.

Everything was laid out to fit into social norms and go to college like everyone else. Problem is I still do not know what I want or going to be.

I'm stuck deciding between two different pathways that I know will take me to different destinations in life. I can't decide what to do. But I do have a successful business and I'm hooked on a drug called being a CEO and designing your business and life in an era where few people did what I did. Now it seems normal to do these days.

As starting college dates approached, my business was in full swing. I still didn't know what my choice of degree should be or what I want to do, but at the time I was gravitating to success types of magazines, like Forbes, Fortune, Success and others.

I was trying to figure out what I wanted to become. Somehow, despite all my lack of education, I was acutely aware at the time that I was a dumb, uneducated kid who needed to learn much. I was self-aware of that.

My father had an extensive library of business motivational books, Napoleon Hill, Earl Nightingale, etc. I raided his library of business books. The Pre-college summer I got a feel for what I wanted and that was to be a business success. But I wanted to have a straight shot at my destiny rather than taking all the classes I'd hated in high school I didn't think I needed.

I decided the CEO bug was mine, and I wanted to build companies and be a CEO of my own someday and that I needed to educate myself. As it came down to the wire to start college, I took a leap of faith and dropped out. Besides, I could always go back to college (I never did).

I canceled the Pell grant and college to attend at a later time if needed. I put it off to see where my new CEO drug took me. I knew I didn't want to work in construction blue collar all my life. Hard labor wasn't my thing, and it's hard to do when you get old. I wanted to be a white collar CEO.

So the next logical step I knew I needed to do was self educate myself for future success. I read all the books and started taking basic MBA lesson orders in the mail from Harvard Business Review, consuming all their magazines as well.

I learned everything I could get my hands on to set up to be a successful CEO and prepared for the time I would make it happen. While I was skipping college, I knew I needed to self-educate myself with my own shaped home taught MBA.

Leadership Lessons:

- Learning To Think Outside The Box
- Scotoma (Blind Spots)
- Vision
- Perspective
- Overcoming Adversity
- Innovation
- Recognizing My Weaknesses
- Self Education
- Work Ethic
- Customer Service
- Challenging and Breaking Models
- Feedback, Adapt and Innovate
- Challenge Social and Business Norms
- Learn From Your Darkest Moments & Grow

5

Gift Of A Lifetime

"You're about to be fired because you can't close deals, I know you're broke, living on Top Ramen, so I'm giving you $10 to go buy "Zig Ziglar's Secrets of Closing the Sale: For Anyone Who Must Get Others to Say Yes!" I know you'll want to buy food but don't, buy the book and read it ASAP."

There are key moments in one's life where one move, one kind gesture can change a life or a lifetime. It is an inflection point where probably neither of you realize it, but at that point, you stand at a fork in the road of life. That gentle gift that someone gives you can change the whole arc of your life. This was one of those moments that changed my whole life and everything that would come.

To this day, I shudder to think about what my life would have been without this seminal fork in my life's road and the path it took me on. Consider this: when you help others, you may never know how far it will take you or them.

After learning the hard lesson that the construction business isn't that fun and business is slow in winter, I needed to add stability and try to augment my income. I was looking for a job to weather the winter and I found a car leasing brokerage that would pay me a draw and help me learn the business. Once again, I was back in the business of sales. The owner's car leasing model was ahead of its time.

As salespeople, we would have to find buyers who wanted an exact car model and color. They would hire us to find that car, negotiate for them to get a deal and then have it delivered to us. Then we would then sell them the car.

I worked there for a couple months until they discovered the owner had not been paying the fees to the banks to cover the vehicle titles.

The owner was also selling auto maintenance policies without paying the auto maintenance companies and never sending in the paperwork. It all melted down when a buyer tried to use his maintenance insurance.

Turns out the owner had been floating over $200,000 worth of cash and contracts that he used to live a lavish lifestyle, including to take him and his new wife's family on a $20,000 cruise. After the news cameras showed up at our office, they fired everyone and I was out of a job. It was crazy! I learned what kiting cash and contracts were and learned not to do it.

So there I was with the only skill of knowing about cars and sales. So I fell right into a job working for a local Chevy dealership for new cars to expand my sales skills. This was interesting, but sadly, I could sell a little, because I didn't have any real great closing skills and you had to sell AND close to make it. I sucked.

So after a couple weeks of trying to make it work, one of my sales managers came to me and said, "Hey man I gotta tell you - most likely you're going to get fired soon, you're not selling and you clearly don't have closing sales skills."

Tony's Sales Lesson #1

His name was Tony. He was this short little guy about five and a half feet who always dressed slick in a suit with a vest. Tony reminded me of a modern day Napoleon. He was always dapper with expensive shoes and a pinky ring. Tony was a real charmer and a charismatic, larger-than-life personality that could be subtle but effective.

After a month of struggling to sell anything, Tony came to me and said, "You're about to be fired because you can't close deals, I know you're broke, living on Top Ramen, so I'm giving you $10 to go buy "Zig Ziglar's Secrets of Closing the Sale: For Anyone Who Must Get Others to Say Yes!" I know you'll want to buy food but don't, buy the book and read it ASAP."

I had always trusted Tony, as he was the nicest manager to me and had taught me many things, so I took his money and bought the book. I knew he had given me a break and my job was on the line. So I crammed, read and soaked up everything Zig Ziglar offered. Learning to "close the deal" was a pivotal moment in my life. I studied all the different closing techniques and mindsets Zig had In the book. It was eye opening.

The next day, Tony asked me if I had bought the book, and I told him I was consuming it. I read the book in 2-3 days and started applying the tools to close the deal. To this day, I'm thankful for what Tony did. It changed my whole life not only as saving me on that job but helping give me the tools to be an entrepreneur.

My life would be very different if not for that simple act of charity. If I recall correctly, I eventually tried to repay him. He refused. It was a magnificent gift, and he knew it was more powerful that way. So right away I employed all the techniques and low and behold I started closing and SELLING! I went from a few sales to lots of sales!

This was one of many seminal moments in my life where one person changed the whole arc of my career. To this day, I fear what I would have been without it. One singular moment of kindness and a gift that changed a lifetime.

Tony had helped me save my job, secured my future, but he'd given me the power to close deals. You know that old saying about teaching a man to fish. I have Tony and Zig Ziglar to thank for it.

Years later, one of my clients who worked with the Zig Ziglar organization in Dallas, Texas, said if I came down to Dallas, they might introduce me to him. I really wish I had done so, since it was on my bucket list for a long time. But I took advantage of the many tapes, CDs, and videos Zig had made. It was a sad day for me when he passed away. I never had time to thank him, so here it is. "Thanks Zig, you changed and saved my life!"

Tony's Sales Lesson #2

I was milling about the showroom one day and Tony came up to me and said, "I'm going to show you something, so pay attention, and pull out your wallet." Then he said "I want you to open it up," so I did. Then he said "Pull that $20 bill out and give it to me." I did and handed it to Tony. He looked at me straight in the eye as he held up my $20. He folded the bill and slid it right into his pocket.

He smiled pleasantly, thanked me and walked off, much to my surprise. Stunned, I said, "Hey wait, where are you going? Do I get my $20 back?" As he kept walking off, he said, "No, YOU GAVE IT TO ME, it's mine now." I stood there, stunned.

Having moved about 20 feet away from me, he stopped and walked back to me. He got in very close to me for affect and to make sure he had my full attention. He said, "I've just taught you one of the most powerful sales lessons ever and I'm keeping the money you gave me so that you will remember this." My mouth dropped.

Then he said, "You GAVE me the money, right?" I replied, "No, you ASKED for the money." He countered, "No, I ASKED no questions. I TOLD you to give me the money."

Still looking confused, he walked me through all of his statements, explaining that he had told me what to do. "Go back through what I told you," as he recounted to me. It became clear he had TOLD me what to do the whole time, through the line of instructions to DO things. There were NO questions.

He had never ASKED for the money, he told me to give it to him and he did it in a way that when he explained it, I had felt like he had never been demanding in his closing, like he'd been asking questions of me the whole time.

He had used my trust in him and closed the deal in the blink of an eye by not asking for the sale, but taking it. He told me if you are acting in the best interests of the client, having built rapport with him/her and giving them what they want, don't ask to close the deal, assume the sale and wrap it up. Don't ASK for the sale, ASSUME IT. CLOSE the sale.

Once he knew I was aware of the lesson and its blueprint to use for myself, he said, "Now I'm going off and keeping what you GAVE me for this lesson." I had to accept that I had just paid for a powerful, important lesson. Still shocked, I couldn't argue with Tony as he walked off to the back service area where the 25 cent coffee machine was.

Tony knew I was a broke kid and later that day he came to me, handed me the $20 and said, "Here kid, I just needed to get your attention so you would remember the power of the lesson, did you learn it?" I had written the money off, but was relieved to get it back. As a lifelong salesperson and sales trainer, the lesson was worth millions.

The lesson was that if you have the client's best interest at heart, don't ask them for the sale outright, take them down a path where they believe they are in control and then sell them what they want that's in their best interests.

A famous salesperson W. Clement Stone was once told by a sales manager: "Boy, as long as you live, never ask a man for his time. Take it!" The lesson: Assume the sale.

Tony's Sales Lesson #3

Tony taught me another great lesson. Tony, as a salesperson, could talk and gain rapport almost instantly with anyone. He had a super firm handshake and would look you in the eye with a gaze of charm that could see right through you. Since he was shorter than most people, he would have to be sharp to grab your attention and hold it.

Tony was a master at entertaining, yet controlling the customer. He was magical at moving his hands to keep people hypnotized. He was like the circus master commanding the attention of any couple he was selling a car to.

One day, he was bragging about flirting with a man's wife right in front of her husband and getting away with it. I asked him how he did it and he said, "You can get away with saying almost anything to anyone, IF YOU SMILE."

There was a lesson. You can be direct with people if you smile. Smiling is everything. You can be mean, tease, lightly insult, etc, if you smile.

One of Tony's sales techniques was when a buyer said no, as in someone's husband, he would use reverse psychology and chink the man's ego a bit in front of his wife. He would say while smiling, "That's okay, you probably can't afford this car anyway, let's go find you a cheaper model that you can afford."

With Tony flirting with his charm on the wife, the husband would take the bait and insist he was man enough to afford it, not wanting to be shown up in front of his wife. Tony would close the deal as the man would buy the deal to prove his manhood.

One of my favorite comedians who could get away with this was Don Rickles. He was a master of being the "insult comedian," but he offended few people. It was because he would smile at you and you knew he was joking. In his voice there was a warm and caring joking love that would come across even though his face might say something else to punctuate the punch of the joke.

Comedians like Lisa Lampanelli and other comedians who can work a room and insult the audience can get away with this principle. Make sure you smile when you sell and gain rapport. It can make all the difference.

Meeting Anthony Robbins

Two great things that came out of the car business while I was studying to be a stockbroker, was meeting Lou Tice in the 9 point box experiment we covered earlier and Anthony Robbins.

I met Anthony Robbins in 1989. He was promoting his book from a few years earlier, "Personal Power". This was a time where he was doing speaking seminars in rooms about the average hotel conference room size. He wasn't a household name at that point. I remember sitting in the front row a few feet from him, and his knowledge and delivery was amazing.

One sales technique he taught us was being exact about setting goals. Robbins would ask people to say what their goals were for the year. Inevitably, someone would say to "make more money." He would toss them a quarter and say, "There you go, you just met your goal."

It was a great lesson that you should write exactly what you want to achieve.

So I did so. Ten years later, I completed my goals, and it turns out I'd met or exceeded all of them.

After the show, people that were interested could freely walk up to him, shake his hand and chat with him, unlike that of his celebrity status today. Totally fired up by his speech, I went up to shake his hand. I'm 6 '1 tall with large hands.

I'll never forget going up to shake his hand and watching my big hand disappear into his far larger, massive hand. Tony is a very prodigious gentleman at 6'7". I was happy to have met him and his knowledge that would change my life.

I don't remember what I said to him but I thanked him…he was very nice. Later, the dealership had Robbins Personal Power CD or tape series you could check out one by one and I consumed it all, later buying a copy for myself from his TV infomercials.

I was looking around for a different career and thought, "what are the top money making industries to shoot for?" In the 80s there were the power industries and jobs on Wall Street, Doctors or Banking. Wall Street was high on the Ivan Boesky "Greed is Good" era, Michael Milken and all the debauchery in the market, so I went to school to become a stockbroker.

During those times studying for the test, I was a facility trainer overseeing a huge dialing facility that housed over 800 dialer terminals and telemarketers per shift owned by Cincinnati Bell. Being a sales trainer was amazing. I designed my curriculum to inspire people using techniques from Anthony Robbins.

An interesting pattern emerged. My trainees were so motivated and skilled after my training, they would hit the telemarketing floor and blow the numbers off all the people who had been working there for a while. I learned much, but I failed the stock broker test the last time by 7 questions.

The brokerage that was hiring me had chosen a cheaper new startup training company. Unfortunately, they hadn't taught us how to break down the double negatives and trick questions on the test. None of us passed the test after 2 tries. I would not be a stockbroker.

CEO Training

My final, what I call my last "CEO training", was working for a company called Feature Films for Families. I ended up working under the CEO named Forrest Baker III. I watched him like a hawk and tried to learn everything I could. He was intriguing for a multitude of reasons.

Unbeknownst to him and me, Forrest was the last key I was searching for in becoming a successful CEO, innovating, and running companies. He held the last tools I needed for my toolbox.

The interesting thing about our journey in life is that sometimes you seem to hit impassable struggles, like you're going nowhere. Wheels seem to keep spinning. It feels like our lives and the future aren't working for us. Feature Films for Families was a company that was selling "cleaned up" "censored" movies to people of faith across the country through telemarketing and mail.

Forrest was a Mormon, and they targeted much of the marketing to religious people around the country who didn't enjoy seeing movies with swearing, gratuitous violence, nudity, and sex in movies.

So his company (much to the chagrin of Hollywood) would edit the movies and sell the copies to these people. It was quite the large operation spanning a couple of enormous office buildings, mostly of telemarketing booths and callers. Since I had worked at Matrixx Marketing/Cincinnati Bell, it was what I knew and had some skill at telemarketing and management.

As CEO, Forrest taught me many things about being a unique and innovative future CEO. One thing Forrest taught me was how to look at systems design and innovate outside of the box.

One of the maddening things about Forrest was his ability to walk into a room or project team struggling with a design, ask a few questions, and then tell you how to make it work or fix it. He could immediately go right to the answer you had been looking for over weeks.

Forrest was an interesting fellow for many other unique reasons. He didn't normally wear suits in the office. He mainly wore a t-shirt, shorts and flip-flops...no CEO ever did that. You showed up to work in a suit or other business attire.

Usually he ate at his desk, so there would be drops of food down the front of his polo shirt over his little potbelly. I'd seen nothing like it. One time, I asked him why he didn't wear a suit to work. He said a suit was too stressful, made him feel pressured, and wasn't comfortable.

Forrest said that since he worked long hours, his mind was just more open and better off, he could be more relaxed, creative, work longer and get stuff done. He said, "Look at my suit wearing, stressed out accountant. He's on his 5th bypass. I don't want to end up like that."

Basically, I had carte blanche to move about the company as an "intrapreneur," searching for improvements and innovations that we could make. I would go into departments and ask questions, of course, such as why do we do things this way or that way.

Testing & Innovating

One day Forrest came to me and said that he wanted me to do an experiment for him to test. As the intrapreneur it was my job to work with innovations with him. He said that he wanted me to take one day and go door-to-door to sell the videos. The company sold everything by telemarketing.

They sent videos through the mail to purchasers. But he said, "I want you to go out and canvas some neighborhoods and see what response you get." Being the testing intrapreneur I said "OKAY."

Now this was not fun. Imagine walking around in a suit like you are some older religious missionary alone, knocking on people's doors in the middle of the day...99% of the people wouldn't open the door for me or weren't home. I would get the usual peek through the curtains and then nothing. A few doors that opened quickly established they were not interested.

What I accomplished was wearing down a hole in my nice dress shoes that must have been getting low already, but the hot pavement and concrete with dress shoes made for the office might not be the best mix for door to door selling. Overall, I drove around to various neighborhoods to get a feel for our testing, but it was an overall failure.

I went back to the office, fairly discouraged. Nothing sold, a few people, vaguely interested, but nothing really happening. Mostly I just walked a lot, knocked on doors, and none opened for me. I talked to Forrest, and he asked how it went.

I explained to him how awful it was. No one opened their doors. Complete failure, complete waste of time. No sales, etc. He looked at me. Matter of fact, he said, "Okay, so it STILL doesn't work." He turned away and went back to whatever he was doing on his computer.

Shocked, I said, "Wait, what did you just say?" "He replied, "Well, it STILL doesn't work." I said to him, "What do you mean it still doesn't work. Have you ever done this before?" He said, "Yeah, a couple of years ago. We did a test where we tried to sell the videos, door to door. What you were testing was to see if, over the last couple of years, things had changed in the marketplace, where it could work. Clearly, it still doesn't work. So, at least we tried, we experimented."

I was aghast, and said, "You just made me walk around for an entire day, knocking on doors in the heat, wearing a hole in my sole. Just to test a theory that you knew would fail?" And he said, "I didn't know it would fail. You're good enough to run this test the right way. I would know whether I would get excellent results if it were possible, so, it still doesn't work, you tried."

This was a very important lesson I learned from Forrest, a very important lesson for innovation, always be testing, always be trying, always be experimenting. Even if something didn't work before, try to see if you can tweak it.

Sometimes it's like a safe. If you can get the perfect combination, you can get something to open up that you couldn't before. Changing a title, changing an angle, changing a place that you might market, or changing to a different newspaper can open a new avenue to success.

There's a million different ways that you can change what you're marketing or doing or building right now. And so the brilliant thing about Forrest was, he would experiment, even if he knew it had failed before he would do experiments, testing different variations, to see if they would work.

And then in the end, I had to go get new soles on my shoes to go with a very important lesson.

Leadership Lessons:

- Don't ASK For The Sale, ASSUME IT. CLOSE The Sale.
- Be an Entrepreneur Or An "Intrapreneur"
- Kiting Cash & Contracts Can Backfire
- Always Be Testing, Trying, Experimenting
- You Can Say Almost Anything If You Smile
- Self Education
- Learning To Think Outside The Box
- Innovation
- Selling & Closing
- Perseverance

6

First Home Run

"This application for a courier license is a POOR application, high on hope and low on substance. IT IS DENIED." Our business dreams seemed dashed. The man who had denied our license was dead wrong. I would prove it through my skill and innovation. That same business model he'd denied would quickly take dominance over the local market and drive two competitors into bankruptcy and others out of business.

Brick And Mortar Business

Since I was 18 years old, I had been running small startup companies trying to find one that had the potential and the right mix that could hit it big. Preparation, practice is everything. Sometimes you start a lot of companies and fail, but you keep learning and then the right moment if you keep seeking might come.

My first successful companies were brick and mortar businesses. They were companies that had to get government licensees, sign office leases, buy furniture and hire employees ALL BEFORE YOU COULD MAKE A DIME.

These were not some "dot com" websites that start selling with a low bar of entry. But a real bootstrap brick and mortar business that we started with literally only $2000. And it HAD to make a profit within MONTHS because we weren't rich enough to lose money like tech startups can.

Then our 2nd company I started a year and a half later with $4000, and I made them both profitable EACH within a few months and built them into multi-million dollar companies that lasted nearly 20 years (and would probably still be here today without the 2008 recession).

Lacking cash flow funds placed us in the gauntlet of businesses that 99% fail in the first 2 years. It was all sweat equity, blood, and tears. This made all the difference between our first business having no debt and a business you could scale by reinvesting the profits immediately.

While working at Feature Films for Families, a friend of mine was working at a major medical reference laboratory that did testing & diagnostics for hospitals and health centers. The company had hired Stat Express Courier Service that used to run "stats" on speedy express trips to hospitals and various clinics.

According to the laboratories staff and my friend there were some other problems with the service and efficiency but the biggest problem was the smoke laden deliveries and drivers. Living in Utah, most of the population was Mormon and smoking is one of their taboos.

Smoke from the chain smoking couriers permeated the packages they were transporting, and a thick cigarette smell would waft around them when they delivered packages into offices. The courier service was the largest, most efficient and well-established business around, but this was a big deal for clients in Utah. People hated working with them, but had to.

Stepping Up To The Plate

So my friend and I decided to start a courier service using the "nonsmokers" incentive for customers. Just that alone was a big competitive advantage that we'd identified. I asked him to work it out on the back end with the lab staff so that we could almost guarantee that we would have their business when we started our company.

I started by analyzing our competition in the industry. One of my friends used to get company secrets from Apple Computers for his Mac magazine by dumpster diving. It was routine corporate espionage back in the day, that even journalists of major news organizations still do. So we both went out to see what Stats Express Courier Company was tossing out into their garbage in the public domain one night.

Most people have learned this, but you can learn another lesson here. Always shred your business documents before you toss them out. Be protective of your information and data. Once you throw something out and put it in the public domain, anyone can get to it and use it. Protect your data as proprietary. Don't tell everyone about your business.

My business partner and I drove out to Stats Express and lo-and-behold everything was in the garbage. We found paperwork printouts of their entire business, out on the curb in a public domain dumpster. I'll never forget how bad it all smelled, especially from all their cigarette butts.

We had all their invoices, their pricing, their P&L's, Balance Sheets, their client list, addresses, phone numbers, the pricing they had with clients…we knew everything. It was insane.

To start our courier company, we had to get registered with the State board that oversaw what they called transportation industries. These State and Federal departments oversaw taxi services, courier services, trucking, airlines, all these different companies that worked in the transportation industry. Transportation companies like ours were regulated locally and sometimes nationally.

This was before Bill Clinton deregulated the industry. So we had to get approval from them to start our new company, Silverstreak Express. The insurance costs they forced on us and the paperwork were off the chart and insanely anal in its formality.

We had to buy expensive commercial insurance per vehicle that was like $3000 a year at the time and was designed for large carriers like FedEx, etc. A hefty hit for a startup company, only running small initial loads of blood & urine samples.

We had to get approved by the Utah Department of Public Service. The application was a bit of a joke with many hoops to jump through. They wanted overvalued income projection balance sheets and profit-and-loss statements that we needed to plan for up to 2 years out. It was crazy.

Especially as a small startup, we didn't know if we were going to make big money or fail outright.

So I put in an honest conservative projection and then submitted all the required paperwork. Then the wait. Like I said, this wasn't the easy business days like now where you just buy a dot com off of GoDaddy and off you go.

Strike 1

When we received a stern denial for our application, it seemed like all our dreams were being shot down. I framed that denial and set it on my back desk for the rest of my career. The letter was brutal: "Compared to others I have reviewed, this is a poor application, difficult to read with little support for financial projections. It is high on hopes and low on substance."

A few other pot shots in the letter were included. The maddeningly insane logic about all of this was they were just pie in the sky projections.

The projections were just that, nothing really based in fact, but there we had to submit it. It was disheartening...a blow to us starting this business that seems like a grand future. But this is what you have to overcome and persevere through. It seemed like there was always someone trying to thwart our attempt at success, and I had to battle or figure out a way to innovate around them. Welcome to the world.

I went down to meet with the gentleman who had denied our application dressed in my suit and business acumen to pull out all the stops to get our application approved. I knew I would not sell this guy on our scrappy little startup sweat equity numbers. I had to sell him using the power of my personality, will, ability to deliver and CLOSE.

I met with him and pulled out all the charm and sales technique stops, he was stunned, along with being a little embarrassed by the harshness of his letter as I read it back to him. In the end, I sold him on our model.

He said we should just turn in some really high projected numbers, even though they were beyond unreal what we would do in the first year. We would then be approved with his blessing. Massive win.

Tony's lessons preparing me to be a great salesperson were everything and the actual key to being a success. Everything I'd learned from Tony, Zig Ziglar, Anthony Robbins all hinged on these important moments. Shortly after all this was done, as agreed, we were approved by the State oversight authority and it was time to launch.

I went to my boss at Feature Films for Families, Forrest Baker III, and told him I would work in the evenings on this other project. I was an "intrapreneur" at his company, and he knew I wanted to be an entrepreneur of my own.

He knew that this was constantly eating at me, and I probably would never be happy until I became a successful entrepreneur, much like him.

When I disclosed to him I would do this side business and probably would just be working my normal nine to five and no longer the extra hours I put in, he made this suggestion. He said, "I'm going to give you two months' pay of your salary to try this project out and get it launched. We use a delivery company called Pony Express, and they're charging us a lot of money.

So maybe if I help you, you will come back to me and I can save some money and get my investment back. But here's the deal. I'm going to give you these two months of income to go do this project. And if this business fails and at the end of that time it does not work out, quit messing around with all these entrepreneurial projects. You need to come work for me. I owe you no more "projects."

Pretty interesting deal to take and have, especially for somebody who wants to get away and start their own business. I enjoyed working for Forrest, but I had the CEO/Entrepreneur bug. I wanted to be like him.

I wanted to work for myself and would never be happy until I did. So I made the deal with them every two weeks, he would have checks for me, just like I normally had been working there, and I would disappear for two months and build my business, and his deal was, is at the end of two months if you have a business, come back to me, we'll see if we can do business together. If not, come back to me and I basically own you. Again, that was the deal, and two-month credit.

In my and my partners spare time, with a lot of sweat equity and using our own vehicles, we launched "Silverstreak Express" the nonsmoking courier service, with me as the CEO and my best friend as the Vice-President.

I came up with our business model, and we were almost ready to go. At the beginning, the two of us would do everything with our own cars, and run around town doing deliveries, trying our best to make money to further build the company.

Thinking it would give us an edge, my friend wanted to drop the pricing down. Unfortunately, he'd never run a business. He did not know how important pricing was, cash flow, or how much any of this stuff is important. All he knew was it sounded like a good idea.

Running a business with this lack of experience would have killed our company so fast. Therefore, I was the CEO, because I'd spent a lot of time running different businesses. I knew the margins were already too small, and we needed to keep as much cash flow as we could. So here was my marketing trick, which was pretty ingenious and if you can use it - try it. IT WAS ABOUT THE LONG GAME.

The Pitch

Since our competitors' pricing was public, I would design a proposal to pitch to our competitors' clients to switch to our service with a saving of $.25 cents per shipment. Now some clients would ship 10+ packages a day so it would add up. I figured out what their ANNUAL COST would be on the $.25 cent saving and scaled it out.

Usually, the long-term savings would be about $1000 a year. That's a big deal and would get people eager to sign on the dotted line. Plus, with my ability to build trust, sell myself and the company, I could close deals, and it helped that we didn't smoke as a bonus.

One of the other brilliant strategies I came up with was how to deal with companies that were secure in not upsetting the apple cart and switching to us. I'd offer this deal clincher just like I had offered the contractors at my first business and it was ballsy: "Try us for 30 days and we'll guarantee you'll be happier with us. If you don't like us, don't pay the bill, it's free and go back to your prior service." A few times, people's jaws hit the floor.

Having that level of confidence from me and my new company was amazing to people, mind blowing and people would sign up over it. Hey, free month of service, what do you have to lose?

That's what leaders do, they stand behind the company and the quality. That always was a deal maker. But people loved the confidence. You don't make that bet if you can't back it up or you're crazy.

As the CEO, I had put my company where my mouth was and built a great company with efficient systems to make sure people were hooked. In all the times we offered the 30 day guarantee, we kept all the clients. In fact, 15 years later, at the end of the company, we had all the same original clients. All from those 2 little sales techniques and, of course, being a better company and giving great customer service.

Early in our business, we had to determine how to set up our billing. When we started, we knew that one of our competing courier companies would bill every two weeks. This was an important find for me because I knew how important cash flow was, especially starting a small business like ours that is self funded. We had a limited time before it would be depleted...money is everything.

Cash flow is almost everything in a business. Especially, our brick and mortar companies with very limited self funding, CASH IS KING.

Unfortunately, my new business partner did not have business experience and demanded that we do 30 day monthly billing instead of every two weeks. Therefore, it is vital to have experienced business people at the head of your companies, even startups. His demand would have been a death knell for us. What I had to explain to him was that if you do 30 days billing, it can take up to 60 to 90 days to get your initial money and if someone defaults on paying their bill, it can take longer.

Most times their bills can be run up further with longer term billing and they can be deep in debt by the time you figure out they will default. This way, if they defaulted, we'd know sooner and have less loss.

Honestly, if someone is going to default on you, the sooner you can figure it out with the lowest losses possible with the least amount of outstanding billing. With two weeks billing, you will start getting your money within the next 15-30 days, which gives you a smaller window of losses and faster cash flow turnaround. This is explosive to your bottom line.

After arguing with my partner, I put my foot down and showed him how much of a difference it would make compared to how fast we would run out of money, and he finally relented.

So there's the thing: don't be locked in by paradigms that you think are rules you have to follow, much like the "thinking outside of the box" many times you can redo the rules. Look for companies that are working outside of the box.

The other problem inexperienced partners have is their temptation to want to be in control. This is a death knell usually. Make sure someone with experience runs the company. We would have been out of business overnight with his lack of experience and demands.

Whether you are starting a business or running a major company with a management team, this is so important to identify and contain these inexperienced people from mucking stuff up. It's better to clarify these things up front and decide whether you want to continue. I see so many people who ignore the initial red flags and they will just amplify. One person needs to lead the company.

We started doing what are called "stat runs", you had to have couriers available 24/7, where they would call us anytime, usually in the middle of the night, and we would have to race to the hospital within a half an hour, pick up the blood, urine or tissue sample race it to the lab within the next half an hour and try to complete the whole process within an hour.

Of course, it was hard on us because we were doing this for a very cheap price. And it was mostly just driving from one place to another. It was interesting work seeing how blood plasma and blood tissue were tested. We started cutting in on Stat Express' clientele.

Our courier business was crazy. In the beginning, we were mainly working with labs and hospitals. Then we discovered that mortgage companies were a better and more profitable business than running emergency stats for ARUP.

Swing For The Fence

We started signing up mortgage companies that had 4-5 offices across the Wasatch Front covering 5 counties. The challenge that we had was the cost of having 5 employees in fleet cars at all the offices in the morning when they opened to deliver the overnight packages and then again before they closed at 5-6 to pick up the overnight packages.

On that schedule, there was no room for showing up late, or vehicle breakdowns. Most of our business had become heavy mortgage folders that were too expensive to send through UPS and Fedex.

Between the two of us starting the company out, we'd spend 12-18 hours driving up and down the area between all the offices. All of our competitors were more established and had plenty of cars and employees, so how could I innovate and stand out?

One problem our clients had was many times when we showed up they were so busy working late to get everything shipped out they would miss the cutoff times we had. Sometimes when we would show up, they would beg us to wait for them, which doesn't work well when you're on a time clock.

In his book, "Thriving on Chaos" Tom Peters talked about a term called "creative swiping." This is where companies "borrow" from one another's ideas and try to make them better. Some might call it stealing ideas, but in his book he termed it "creative swiping."

As someone who keeps their eyes open, watching for opportunities and innovations, I came across a smaller courier company that was successful in California. They used smaller drop boxes similar to UPS, FedEx & USPS, but custom placed at offices with a lock and key.

The Home Run

I researched how we could buy some small lock boxes to chain down and to be hidden on our client's office properties. Then the innovation came together in my head. If we put these drop lock boxes on every client's outdoor property, they could put their packages in them at night and they could retrieve their received packages in the morning from the box. It was brilliant.

We could go from up to 5 employees needing to be at everyone's offices in

5 counties both morning and night to just one employee doing it all. They would drive up and down the Wasatch Front and hit all the offices, picking up and dropping off at the same time. We could do it in one swooping run.

Silverstreak could then deliver any deliveries that went to 3rd party offices like Countrywide or other places by a 2nd courier in the mornings. Eventually, we partnered with all the major players.

It would give our clients more time to work later and get their packages shipped. It was customer service and innovation at its finest. So I approached my clients and sold them on the idea. They had gotten to know and trust us. Some of our favorite clients just gave us keys to their office, and we bonded our couriers for security.

Imagine going from the cost of having 5 employee manned fleet cars all day long to just one employee fleet car at night, doing the same revenue as the 5. Cost was now 5 times lower between cars and employees, less car maintenance costs and at least 5 times more profitable for the same revenue.

The courier was traveling at night so less traffic, less potential for accidents, it was brilliant. And our clients were ecstatic they would work sometime late into the evening and still catch the driver coming through around midnight. In the middle of the night, one driver could run the whole route.

I had achieved massive cost savings while increasing the benefits to our customers with a system so good they couldn't leave.

Not one of our competitors in the local market could understand what I had innovated, and we slowly took over the mortgage market. We became known as the great invisible courier. They would for years never see our couriers, just put the packages in the lockbox to go out and in the morning, their deliveries were there like magic.

Sometimes our customers would call and joke about how we were so consistent but had never met us. Some customers never met us for over a decade. We'd set their account up. In the middle of the night, we would place a mailbox at their office with the keys slid through their mail slot. And then we'd begin.

One of the other advantages was the packages were usually in the boxes around 3 am. So instead of waiting till 9-10 for most delivery trucks, they could grab their deliveries and start whatever processing work they needed as soon as employees arrived in the morning. It made more jobs for our customers' employees as well as they advanced their hours to 6 am to start earlier.

It was exceptional and not one of our competitors caught on. They were still locked "inside the box" of their old business model for deliveries. We became so loved that as employees moved around to different employers, they would tell their new company about our amazing innovative service and help us land them as a client. We had an army of loyal, loving customers being our evangelists, bringing us new clients.

The loyalty was off the charts. With the service we provided, no one could match us. Trying to beat us on price didn't matter. You couldn't steal our clients unless you offered our same service. Since it was so cost effective for us, you couldn't beat our prices either.

The one cool thing about our company was we operated like clockwork with my innovative overnight routes, and it gave us time to fix problems without our clients being any wiser. Mostly, day in and night out, it operated like a well-oiled machine. A car could break down in the middle of the night and still leave us hours to save the shipment and keep on trucking.

Superior Customer Service

How you handle customers is everything, and the response is super important. Every few years, we would screw up. A complaint call would come in from our courier company. I would tell the client how much we appreciated their business and then give them the entire month off for free. The client would be in shock because it was a huge refund for their company.

I would tell the client that their business was that important to us. I wanted them to know how much we valued their business and loyalty. The response was massive loyalty, and people rarely left. When a few left, they would soon be back. No one could compete with us. We took so much business away from our competitors and became the dominant force.

We scaled so fast that 2 competitors filed for bankruptcy and others laid-off employees in the local market. I was amazed no one ever figured it out, but no one could see outside of the box they had made locked into the business "norms."

Amazingly, 15 years later, when I had moved to Vegas and shut down the company, almost all of our original core of clients I had signed up for the first 6 months had been with us all those years. I just would pinch myself all the time at how wonderful it was.

Overall, we went all those years with far fewer employees and costs than any other courier company. A brick and mortar company built with $2000, achieved profitability within 3-4 months and within one and a half years, gave me the ability and time to start our second company Park Place Mortgage. That laid a foundation for so many companies after that.

The Cherry On Top

About 6 months after leaving with my two-month salary gift from Forrest Baker III, we took his deal to replace his current courier with our service. He became our top customer for the next 5-6 years. So not only did he help us launch Silverstreak Express, he became a top customer.

Later, I would employ his software programmer, who had built his phone systems to build my mortgage company a massive phone dialer for telemarketing. The value of the win was extraordinary. A long-term vision is everything.

Thanks Forrest for the gift you gave me.

Leadership Lessons:

- Seek Competitive Advantages
- Preparation, Practice is Everything
- Customer Service
- Cash Flow Is King
- Dont Price Yourself Short

- Control Inexperienced Partners
- Only One Person Can Lead
- Analyze Your Competitors Know Their Weaknesses
- Innovation
- Overcoming Adversity
- Courage
- Perseverance
- Vision
- Challenging and Breaking Models
- Learning from Rejection and Failure

7

A Boy, a Log, a Piece of Tin And Greedy Vermin

"I'm not stuck in a lawsuit with you. YOU'RE STUCK IN A LAWSUIT WITH ME," I said to the business plaintiff, who had sued my company for $300,000.

This is a legal lesson about one of the most important stories I ever learned that gave me an outside of the box perspective that saved me in lawsuits, as a business entrepreneur, and life lessons. All because of one story, in a book I read as a child. This one story saved me a lot of money and pain and now lets see if it can help you. Save this story if you're ever in a legal business suit and it's a good parable for dealing with life's lessons.

One thing that you find when you become successful and you get "rich" is that big businesses and rich people use lawsuits for business and financial war. No one raids your castle anymore with a teaming army of sweaty warriors. It's all done by slick, well dressed suited attorneys and court filings.

As a successful business, you find many people will try to shake you down with lawsuits, settlement demands or just hit you up to borrow money all the time.

So many years ago, after starting our first two major companies, we started another company, an acting and modeling agency, with the help of one of our loan officers who knew the business. The TV show "Touched by an Angel" was the number one rated show on television and they filmed it in Utah.

A massive writers' strike in Hollywood had driven TV & Film production to other states like Utah because of their open anti-union stance and welcoming business arms.

It was a great time to take advantage of this boom. After starting up, we hired a guy with the nickname "Shaun-blue" who had worked at a competing agency for a while and left. The agency he had come from was one of the biggest agencies in the valley.

Shortly after that, two employees came to us that had left the same competing agency. There had been several alleged unethical (or worse) behaviors from the prior agency and the employees hadn't gotten their last paychecks. We hired them.

Shortly after hiring them, I got a call from the owner of their prior employment's competing agency. She started talking to me about myself and what we were doing with our agency, following it with an invitation to meet up for lunch or dinner. I thought it might be an excellent opportunity to talk to her about buying her out since my employees had told me several, let's say, "curious" unethical stories.

So I brought it up on the call as if she might consider talking about me buying her company out and she seemed to be interested in it. We agreed to go to my favorite dinner place, the local oyster bar. She asked to get picked up at her office, and I agreed, as I could control the frame to buy her out or negotiate a deal.

One major issue with her was that she was "rumored" to be an extreme pathological liar. My employees had given me the rundown of her way of operating and doing things, such as monstrous claims of her being on the cover of Vogue more than anyone.

No one, of course, had ever seen the covers, always bragging about it. The list of misnomers & stories she told was over the top. Her ex-employees disclosed some stories of how she allegedly used to rip people off...she would buy their goods or services up to $5000 and then claim her Amex card had been stolen. She would keep the merchandise while AMEX would return the money. Lots of evil games, if true. The alleged stories were endless.

The Strange Acquisition Meeting

I left for the dinner prepared by her ex-employees on the trap doors I was walking into. As far as I knew, I was going to a business meeting to discuss a buyout or merger with our companies and size up the competition.

So I went to dinner with the competitor. At the dinner we had a pleasant talk. I wanted to find out the value of her company in her mind, and what options were on the table. For most of the time, she talked and flirted with me and she told me the most outlandish "stories" that clearly weren't truthful. I think in all the times someone has ever lied to me openly, this had to be the most outrageous bold faced lies I've ever seen.

One lie was that her little side hustle printing coupons for companies in the local free Big Nickel & other free classifieds, was that one of her biggest clients was the company Firestone and that she ran ALL the national advertising for the company. I replied, "Wow, you run national TV, newspaper & radio advertising for them? The answer was "yes." I had to work hard not to have my jaw hit the floor.

I don't know how stupid she thought I was, but being very familiar with the advertising powerhouses of the "Big 5" and "Madison Avenue" her lies were laughably extreme.

There were some other extraordinary lies she told me that made me so uncomfortable along with the story of the 3 years she's spent in courts fighting with the parent of her child, a rich guy in Florida.

She was a legislative nightmare that verified all her ex-employees' warnings. I wrapped the dinner and left. I had no interest in buying a business from this person as she couldn't be trusted, and I'd met no one who could tell such tall tales to people like that.

So I took her back and dropped her off at her place. She invited me in to see her office, but I needed to get away from her as fast as I could. I went back and briefed her ex-employees, my new ones, and we all figured it was best to move onward.

Then it got weird. Very weird. Did I mention VERY WEIRD?

The next day, I got a call from a mutual friend of my company and hers. He started asking me how the DATE had gone. "DATE?" I asked. He said, "I hooked you both up and told her you two should date, so she was going to call you and go to dinner. You guys went, right?" I was shocked.

My brain reeled. Holy moly, my friend had set us up for a date. My friend hadn't told me and I thought I was going to a business meeting.

WOW. Not only would I have had no interest in her from what her ex-employees had told me, the information I learned at dinner was beyond the pale. This was a type of person I'd want nothing to do anything with in my private life.

Given I would never call her back, little did I know this would end up falling into the category of "hell hath no fury like a woman scorned." All her employees had been at her office when I picked her up and dropped her off and she had bragged about it.

Turns out I would live to regret it BUT learn some very important legal and life lessons that actually for what it cost me in the end was fairly cheap financially but precious in the end.

Extortion

I continued to build the talent agency, along with my mortgage & courier company. About a month after this confusing "date", we were served with a massive lawsuit for $300,000. The lawsuit was largely because we'd hired 2 ex-employees that had a non-compete agreement with the company owner I'd gone on the "date" with.

The suit also claimed the first employee we'd initially hired, "Shaun-blue", had also signed a non-compete agreement even though he hadn't.

Upon getting served, we wrapped up and shut down the new company, sealing it off from any income it might receive. It had zero assets as the furniture and other assets were on loan from our mortgage company and because it was brand new; it was operating at a loss.

They had literally just sued a new company, with no income or assets. Then we reopened the business under another name and kept on trucking. So basically a brilliant strategy was to seal up the company with no assets or any continuing income.

So we went into the courts for the injunctive process of a few initial hearings to have a judge determine if there was enough evidence to deem the lawsuit worthy as valid and allow it to continue. It was 4 days of testimony.

Almost comically, they subpoenaed our friend who had tried to get us together for the "date" and he actually testified on the stand of him attempting to do that. It was almost comedic if it wasn't so sad.

And at the end of the injunctive hearing, the judge awarded the plaintiff, and the court ordered us to release the two employees. But the first employee we had hired "Shaun-Blue" had no non-compete agreement and he could keep working with us.

We complied and hired them to work for the new company under the guise of our mortgage company. So in the end, we just kept on trucking. Word came down from the attorneys that it really ticked her off that one employee had gotten away and could still work for us.

The Shakedown

At that point we were going to a full lawsuit and then came the shakedown offers, which was the whole intent of it all. They wrote us an offer to settle, which stated we had to fire all the employees, close the business and agree to never get back into that business to compete with her.

The offer was to pay $50,000 for her attorney fees so far in the suit. It was a tall order. Based on the amount their attorney costs had added up between preparing the lawsuit and hiring the $1200 an hour attorneys, she'd racked up costs extraordinarily fast.

Lesson: What most people don't know is a secret in lawsuits. It costs more to sue someone than defending a lawsuit. There is more work and cost involved for the plaintiff. This is an important thing to learn.

So with an offer to settle, I had to take an inventory of the situation. Up to that point, we had spent almost $10,000 with our attorneys. The opposing plaintiff, had spent $50,000. Just to get the injunction, their litigation was 5 times the burn rate of our burn rate. Since we were up for $300,000 in losses, we had to consider what to do, settle for $50,000 or gamble $300,000 and years of litigation.

So I asked my attorney if we proceeded with the lawsuit about how much it would cost. I had to evaluate what the cost could run against for the risk of losing or winning long term or the short-term cost.

My attorneys told me that the full cost over 2-3 years to do the lawsuit would be about 5 times the amount that we had spent so far. So basically, if I ran the entire course, she would have to spend $250,000 of her money and we'd have spent $50,000 to defend ourselves.

So the question is, do I give her $50,000 NOW or roll the dice on the same $50,000 to play out the case where she would have to spend $250,000 to prosecute it, hoping to win $300,000. And did she have it? According to her ex-employees, she did not. But with risk anything can happen.

I was definitely having a hard time deciding what to do. But the employees that we had hired knew she didn't have the money. This was a shakedown lawsuit and mostly to shut us down from competing with her. So I was thinking she didn't have the money to sink into a full 3 years.

I remember feeling really pummeled by what could be a major decision on the action I chose.

Do we take the loss or gamble? I pondered relentlessly on what to do. My attorneys, of course, wanted to move forward and spend all my money. I wanted it to end.

I pondered over the idea that she had TRAPPED me in this lawsuit and there was no way to get out. It was a weird place to be. I had never been caught in something that had me tied up like this. I had considered trying to get my attorneys to offer a counteroffer, but they didn't want to.

A Boy, a Log, a Piece of Tin and A Greedy Vermin

I really centered on the "trap" I was in. Then suddenly it came to me, a story that I remembered from a book I read as a kid. The book was "Where The Red Fern Grows." This ended up being the single most important paradigm that saved me in this lawsuit and many other things one can learn about business and life.

In the book "Where The Red Fern Grows" there is a story about a young boy who traps or trees raccoons with hounds. The boy did this mainly for their skin in a time where you had to do that to survive for meat and fur trade. One of the key stories in the book is "treeing" whereby the hounds chase the animal up into a tree, trapping it. But shooting the raccoon out of a tree or trapping it with a steel trap would damage the fur.

In the book, the young boy comes up with a way to trap them without damaging the fur. The story goes he bore out a small hole in a log. The inside of the hole was WIDER than the opening to the hole. Then a small square piece of shiny tin was put into the hole, barely big enough to get into the hole's entrance.

The concept is that the raccoon would come along with their curious nature and see the shiny piece of tin, stick their paw into the hole that will barely fit their hand. When they wrap their paw around the shiny tin, they cannot remove their expanded fingers from the smaller entrance hole.

They are trapped as long as they hold on to the tin piece. Now here's the rub - the raccoon could easily give up the piece of tin. It could just simply open its hand, drop the tin, pull its hand out and escape the approaching hunter who laid the trap.

The young boy in the book discovers he can actually walk right up to the raccoon and with one fatal blow end its life. The stubborn raccoon will go to its death in a total attempt it cannot override, to relinquish that piece of tin. It will die trying to hold on to something it cannot take with it after. Total Suicidal Greed.

There are many life and business lessons in this book, but the epiphany I had was they did not trap me in a lawsuit with her. They trapped her in a lawsuit with me. Not only could I not wiggle out of her lawsuit, but I could opt to not let her out of her trap without MY permission to settle. Both parties have to agree to settle to end it.

We were both trapped. This totally changed the dynamic of my perspective. I'm not trapped in a lawsuit with you, you are trapped in a lawsuit with me.

Paradigm Negotiating

This gave me a whole new paradigm to negotiate the lawsuit. I realized I was not the raccoon; SHE WAS. She had launched an assault on my company that could cost her $250,000 to fight that she likely didn't have. I realized I wasn't powerless in the settlement negotiations and having that frame CHANGED EVERYTHING.

If I told my attorney let's go full throttle, she would have to pony up a 2-3 year bleed out of $250,000 in the gamble that she would win and recoup the money. Or she could lose because she was gambling as well. If she lost or ran out of money and had to settle, two-three years from now, I'd be out up to $50,000.

Pay the money now or gamble for later? Now we had a game on and with my raccoon story perspective, I had her trapped in her moment of greed. She couldn't get out without my permission.

I went back to my attorneys and told them to make the following counter offer: For $15,000 in payment to me, I would LET HER out of HER lawsuit. I would keep being in the business, I'd keep all the employees and they would pay their own attorney fees.

My attorneys were beside themselves. They were horrible negotiators. Many are. I told them to write it or I would fire them and find attorneys that would. They complied. A key lesson here: always manage your attorney and attempt to be smarter than them.

Always shop around for the best attorneys who can negotiate and have a perspective on lowering your costs and get suits over quickly.

The court and attorney work is a multitude of procedure hearings and maneuvers that can bleed your money dry. Don't use them blindly. Ask all the hard questions, use strategy, manage the process. Don't be afraid to fire them.

Manage them like you would your business. Hire well, understand everything, strategize the process. Shortly after I settled this, I fired all of them. Many times you can do the procedures yourself for minor matters. For bigger lawsuits, hire them to consult or work the case.

The key to negotiations is to start on the far outside of what you really want to settle on and move inward to where you wanted to be all along. I wanted to get out with as little cost as I could, if any at all. I also wanted to establish a powerful belief in my position to be like a sledgehammer coming down. It had to be shock worthy.

For the counteroffer, I also sent them a mental bomb. I told them they had sued a C-Corporation which by law shielded our personal assets from the business suit. We communicated I wasn't worried about me and my partner's personal assets. They could have the old company for all I cared about. We had sealed and shut down the company at the service of the lawsuit.

Another important lesson to know… attorneys, when they go to sue someone, they look for ASSETS. They don't enjoy hearing there aren't assets of cash, property, anything sizable or lien-able assets on the defendant.

If they don't have that guaranteed return of getting money out of the defendant, they will demand from their client a larger retainer fee since they know even if they win, they'll have trouble collecting on a lack of assets. So they put the burden on the plaintiff, who hired them to pay a higher retainer.

This is a super important lesson in winning court cases. It's why we had shut down the corp as soon as we got sued so it wouldn't develop any assets or cash revenue. Being a few months old, it operated at a loss. I knew that the "bomb" I was sending over was that her attorneys would then demand more retainer from her.

In the counteroffer, I pointed this all out to them. They had sued an asset-less C-corp that we'd shut down and moved the employees to another company. Honestly, they could just keep playing whack-a-mole for a lifetime suing all companies. We'd keep moving them too as they bled themselves out of funds.

Then I gave them the hard math. At their 5 times burn rate, I had only spent $10,000 to their $50,000, which meant they would spend the next 2-3 years burning up $250,000 compared to up to $50,000 for me. So when choosing whether I should settle to pay her $50,000 now OR pay out the $50,000 for the next 2-3 years, I bet she didn't have the $250,000 to pay out the lawsuit, so I'D RATHER GO ALL THE WAY.

I want to see you spend $250,000. I'm not stuck in a lawsuit with you, you're TRAPPED in one with me so enjoy the burn rate.

Again, once her attorney saw this, they would hit her up for higher retainers, encouraging her to settle or pay up. It was a risk, but a good bet considering I'd studied her assets and her ex-employees had told me much about her finances.

So the counter offer went back. $15,000 in payment to me. I would keep being in the business. I'd keep all the employees and they would pay their own attorney's fees. I expected that as soon as their lawyers saw the counter offer, they would crap themselves.

Plus, it was a ballsy move that would make an explosive statement, as my attorneys told me no one negotiates like that. No one but me in this case (always think outside the box).

I was dead on. They freaked out. Somehow, no one had figured out that it was a C-corp, so they thought our assets were exposed. They were not. Incredible tactical oversight error. That would have been the first thing I'd checked what their business model was for liability.

This is the very reason I'd chosen a C-Corp and the payoff day had arrived. Not to mention it is almost silly to sue a brand new company, but she probably thought it had assets and money invested. Instead, it was just furniture and cash lines from our other company and we funded it monthly.

Swift and desperate, their counter offer came back. I would have at least waited a week to not seem desperate. It told me everything I'd gambled on was correct. In it they demanded we pay them $25,000 and walk with the aforementioned release of employees and business bans.

I countered back another power position: I would accept $10,000 down from the $15,000 under the same conditions. This strategy cemented more of my confidence in being communicated to them. I had a powerful hand.

Here's the other key: at this point she was bleeding more massive $1200 an hour attorney fees just for the back and forth. She was trying to stop the bleeding. I was fine since it cost me 5 times less for everything. "You can pay me to get out of your trap, Ms. Raccoon."

They countered back again $10,000. We had to leave the business and fire the employees.

I countered back what I originally had strategized I could get to: they pay their attorney fees; we pay ours and this is over; we don't leave the business; we had already removed their ex-employees, but them working for our other companies that were not in the lawsuit wasn't negotiable and having them work for our other companies was not in the lawsuit and therefore not negotiable.

I'd ground them down. They took the offer in a heartbeat. And I smiled. Overall, in the attorney discussions, they had run up a tab of greed of $50,000 while we got out with $10,000. Not a bad cost for a precious lesson I would use again and again in my life, not only in lawsuits but in all aspects.

Karma

Realizing I had option and power in her trap empowered me to make my moves and essentially win against a brutal bully. We kept the employees and built a competing, successful modeling & acting agency under the new company and name. She failed to stop me and created an even bigger monster with my resolve.

It made me work harder to beat her in the competitive market. The company ran for 6 years until I got bored and moved out of State and made us a ton of money. In fact, the billable made a nice residual income for me up to 8 years later.

A short while later, my attorney came to me with the news that she had tried to default on the payment to her attorneys. Engaging in her same modus operandi she always did by complaining to people trying to get their bills reduced after she had gotten their services, as with her AMEX card.

She had tried to cut them down to $25-35,000, and they sued her and put a lien on her assets. Not a smart thing to do with powerful attorneys. We sat and had a massive laugh.

Another lesson, normally when you contract with an attorney, the contract says they can lien your assets to get paid. You always want to pay your attorneys.

Years later, her alleged unethical ways would lead her to be sued by the Utah Department of Consumer Protection, which she settled for $40,000 dollars followed by bad publicity coverage of it on TV and newspaper. She later closed her company and moved out of state, then filed bankruptcy for $364,000. Karma is sweet.

I would really have been screwed if I hadn't thought outside of my attorney's box and paradigms. Who knows how much money and damage it would have cost me. All from the power of a story I remembered, in a book I read multiple times as a kid: "Where the Red Fern Grows." A little boy, a log, a piece of tin and a damned greedy vermin.

Leadership Lessons:

- Powerful Negotiation Tactics
- Paradigm Shifts
- Thinking Out of the Box
- Perseverance
- Vision
- Willpower
- Manage Your Attorneys - Understand the Process
- "Where the Red Fern Grows" Raccoon Lesson - Don't Let Greed Take You To Your Death

8

Why Entrepreneurs Usually Fail

"Failure is not fatal, but failure to change might be." - John Wooden

Why do so many entrepreneurs fail, and what can we learn from their failure? My favorite book, "Where The Red Fern Grows" demonstrates why.

I had reached a point in our **businesses where** I didn't love what I was doing and I had gotten bored. Personally, I was feeling uninspired. When you don't love the business that you're in, it's hard to go to that next level. Which is why I recommend finding something you love to do first.

I had formed a nice little empire of three core companies and a bunch of small company side projects...I kept trying to add a fourth big one to our little empire of solid companies. The mortgage business was significant money, but I was tired of its cyclical nature based on interest rates. I'd burned out by watching seesawing markets of our mortgage rates that would burn up potential profits in our pending closing portfolios.

Over the course of two major events, I had literally seen our money evaporate in profits almost $400,000 over some Russian policy blowing up and market volatility. The week before 9-11, we lost $75,000 over two days and that gets to you. We never lost money. It would strip away just the profit cream.

Rates up, rates down, business up and down. Ugh. No matter how hard you worked the mortgage business, the market controlled it no matter how perfect the model and would still go up and down based on rates. I ALWAYS FELT BETRAYED.

The courier business was just a revenue stream for myself at high risk if one of our cars ever injured or killed someone on the highway. I had looked many times(**in**) **at** making it a multi-State company like our mortgage company, but the long routes leading out of central Utah to connect didn't make financial sense to run.

There was more return on investment value in working on the mortgage branches. The Acting & Modeling business was just mainly an ego project that made money, was fun, but mostly gave me a nightlife of clubs and events like the Sundance Film Festival.

I was still looking for a business I truly loved, that rocket ship that would take off and hold sustainability. Something that could go huge nationwide and viral. But it was too hard to do with our little trusted core of a two-man management team with my Vice-President and I. We'd invested in a lot of little side products, but didn't have the focus and time to put into them.

For all my years in business, I had tried to find a competent third manager who could build out as a partner for us. We had a fairly good one who ran our courier company, but he was a laid-back guy who wasn't up to our tier. Most of the top earners and players in my companies were salespeople, and they rarely made skilled managers. Plus, I needed someone loyal I could trust beyond a shadow of doubt, like my partner.

The Acquisition Idea

So I was talking one day with one of my friends who was a business broker and he gave me an incredible idea.

The dirty secret of both business and residential real estate brokers is that they see all the best deals first in their exposure to sellers coming to them and working with other agents. The deals that are coming to market that have the best value, agents will scoop up the deals for themselves before they are listed.

So my business broker friend taught me that when he'd find someone in trouble or having a hard time business wise, needed to sell their business or take on investors as brokers, they would see the business first. Many times the company had assets that had been mismanaged and were therefore "asset rich & cash poor."

When my business broker friends would buy them out of their business, many times the assets were worth more than the buy out cost, enriching my business broker friends. Most businesses weren't worth saving, and some had a chance if the assets, business or employees could be folded into successful companies like ours with a better management team.

I don't know where I came up with running an ad for business loans. Maybe I could find companies like ours and buyout/merge/takeover their businesses in a "white knight" scenario bailing out entrepreneurs standing at the face of filing bankruptcy.

The beautiful part was it didn't require me to start a business. Basically, depending on the deal, one of our companies would do the deal or we personally would do it out of our pockets. Or the company could fold into one of ours or we'd get some great office furniture.

The market was in small companies run by entrepreneurs who had been running a business for a while, gotten successful and then fell on hard times. Preferably, asset rich, cash poor.

Need Cash?

I started running ads in the paper for "Money To Loan - Are you a business in trouble? Who needs a loan or investors to help? Call us at…" something to that effect. It worked amazingly well. It flooded us with entrepreneurs in trouble of all sizes and the best part of it, we could cherry pick the deals we wanted. Just sit back and choose the right deal. It was brilliant.

The other mind blowing thing is when we would ask for financial P&L's and Balance Sheets, people would send them right over to us. "It would blow my mind" I was shocked how quickly people would share them. Just amazing.

For any company in business right now, if you walked into it and asked to see the books, they would tell you a hard "NO." Yet for our "money to loan" business, they would send them to us willingly and without Non-Disclosure Agreements.

We could see everything about the business, ask questions and sit back and cherry pick. I knew how much money they wanted to borrow to bail them out, what the worth of their company was, and how they were bleeding out. Most of the companies that came to us were within 6 months to a year of going out of business. They were surviving on fumes and personal credit lines.

Hard rule in business, if you're not growing you're dying. It's hard to recover from a business failing at a certain point.

Once I found a company that I could either possibly turn around or fold the assets or employees into our business,' I would do a call with the entrepreneur. Then, if it looked promising, it was time to go meet with them and tour their business.

Most of the time, it would be an entrepreneur who was still using the original business model he'd started with. He'd had a windfall of cash or loans to start it and the model worked for maybe a short while, or he thought it did. He'd still be stuck in the same model box, trying to beat it to death as his business ran into the ground. Other times, it was an entrepreneur that had a solid business model for years and then the market had changed and he ran that model out of sync with the times, eventually killing his business.

I would go out to tour their business, and that's where it usually got interesting. When I'd go see their operations, and it was obvious why they were failing the moment I walked in the door. Many times we'd find family members working there. Often we'd find their family working at the business.

They usually had employees I'd never hire. In fact, most of the entrepreneurs wouldn't even be people I'd hire based on their lack of business acumen. Sloppy setups without modern business techniques or equipment.

So after touring their office and deciding if it was savable, I'd sit down with them and make them an offer. The offer would always be to remove the biggest problem from the business and what was causing it to fail: I had to remove the entrepreneur.

The fundamental asset or problem for a savable business IS the en-

trepreneur. Remove the problem and take over the company. It's the same
principle when corporate raiders take over a broken company and remove
the problem at the core. There are many reasons to do this.

You're going to be taking their "baby" and changing everything, sometimes
folding it into yours or totally reworking it. One challenge is they will still
think the company is theirs and they will just fight and sabotage you as you
try to make massive changes.

You're going to take their company in an entirely different direction and
instead of the incompetent management that got them there, you're going to
inject a better business model, disrupt and reroute everything.

Anytime I'd make an offer, 100% of the time I'm offering them a buyout.
But here's the rub - they have usually run this thing into the ground and are
within 6 months of filing bankruptcy.

The Offers

The offer I'll make is: Look, you're on your way to bankruptcy and from
what I can see, you are going out of business. Giving a loan is a bad idea, but
I can help you. If you file bankruptcy, you'll wipe out your credit, you'll hurt
your wife and family and likely lose it all. What I'm going to do is bail you
out of your prison here.

I'm going to save you from having to file for bankruptcy and save your
credit and family from hitting the wall. I'm going to take over your business
& assets and since your business is broke, here's what I will give you for
"walking money" (depending on the assets value I'd offer them $1000, $5000,
$10000).

Usually it was just a few grand of walking money. The company is broke
and will require us to flood it with cash to fix it and usually get past due
accounts and landlords out of arrears. Hence the walking money.

Questions would usually arise, such as asking if I would keep their family
they had hired as employees - that was always a BIG NO. Family is almost
100% awful. You need people who know they can be fired the moment they
are a problem. So I would usually tell them that many of their employees

would be likely to go once I took over.

That usually was a struggle for them as one reason their business was failing was they weren't running a business with employees, they were running a business with friends/family who between their poor management and the employees playing the friend/family card were many times ruining the business.

Also, leaving their business behind was a struggle for them. You're asking someone to give up their dream and they usually lack the business experience to see they are about to hit the wall.

They live in this dream state, thinking just maybe they can bail it out or some trick will save them. They don't understand running a business is a whole complex network of standards, policies and competent management techniques at play. It's not the turn of a friendly poker card.

I would have to beat them down a bit that they had to leave, but I was saving them and their credit and probably their family. In financial crises, divorces often happen and there is more to lose than just a failing business if you file bankruptcy.

The failing entrepreneurs would be thrown out because I could see potential in their business and they would think somehow they could figure out what my trick pony was and how to save it. The problem is they didn't have the resources, the experience or ability to see outside of the box like I could. A large part of the time they would deny me taking it over.

When we could do a deal, it was great. We could gain excellent businesses or assets, usually to fold into ours.

"Where The Red Fern Grows" Lesson Again

Guess what would usually happen? I would have to say, why don't you think about my offer, then I would have them sign a first right of refusal document and give them $10 for legal consideration.

They would sign the contract basically under the first right of refusal premise that I would be the first person they would call when they wanted to sell or turnover the business.

Sometimes this would work, but I would have to read them the riot act: "Don't call me a week before you're about to file bankruptcy. I can't save you then. You want to be calling me in a week or two."

Sadly 99% of the time they would call me right before they were about to file their bankruptcy. You couldn't beat the level of stupidity. But this is how they got there and where the lesson of the raccoon who won't let go of that piece of tin in "Where the Red Fern Grows" and hanging on will kill them.

Over the course of my business, I would constantly come into contact with entrepreneurs who massively failed with their models and interestingly enough, they would have more money than I when they started their company.

If you remember, I turned a $4000 investment into a multi-million dollar company that lived for almost 20 years until the 2008 mortgage business collapse.

One day I was interviewing guys for my mortgage salesperson position., and he told me how he had come into an easy windfall of $200,000. He then sunk all that money into starting a mortgage company.

Unlike me and the cheap way we leased our Class C offices for our companies, that we could expand and control, he went out and literally got the HIGHEST COST Class A office space in town. The highest commanding office complex in the valley per square foot cost.

He told me he figured that would flood in the business with the elite offices. Then, while we bought cheap furniture for the areas of our company, customers didn't see, he bought all the nicest, most expensive furniture. Like REALLY expensive.

Then he hired and paid top dollar for mortgage salespeople with high draws, salaries, etc. Instead of starting small and scaling, he went all out. Spending massive amounts of money paying top dollar for everything he thought would bring all the business flooding in.

Having spent all the $200,000, he was now broke and out of business in 1.5 years. And here he was sitting and asking for a job from me. As we talked, he was also perplexed how we could stay in business in our old scruffy Class-C building. He couldn't figure out how we had survived 10 years. I didn't hire him.

He was an owner, not a salesperson. One thing that stuck out to me was I was a salesperson first and then an owner. That's what made me a good CEO. He wasn't.

Where The Red Fern Grows Business Lesson: In every case these entrepreneurs were failing because they'd come up with an original model and then, while maybe that model worked or didn't, they had almost fully blown through all their money and were facing bankruptcy within the first few months.

That or they had a viable business with a suitable business model for years, but the market had changed on them and they had not adjusted their model.

Just like that raccoon who wouldn't let go of the shiny tin, the entrepreneur wouldn't give up that business model even though it was running them into the ground. They would just keep holding on to that business model until it grinds to a full halt. They are usually so confused and can't see outside the box they made.

Off they'd go to bankruptcy, and as I had reminded them, do not call me at the last second. They'd blown their chance. Never look a gift horse in the mouth.

Again, this was the major problem I saw after auditing tons of applications and business that applied and came in contact with over the years. Entrepreneurs couldn't see another model outside of their boxed in views and would never change.

Many times I had to reconfigure our models and when I didn't, it ended up being a painful financial lesson. In the next chapters, we'll talk about techniques to avoid this from happening to you and your business and how to innovate and upgrade your business models.

Don't be the business raccoon who meets his death clutching until the very end of an outdated business model. You need to adjust as you go and constantly be tweaking and adjusting your model BEFORE the market forces you to change.

And like many successful businesses that innovate, sometimes you can create something that fully destroys your current business model but creates a new one that is more sustainable for future markets. Many times this is called "Eating your own lunch."

Another Business Lesson

One of my mortgage business vendors was a credit reporting agency that pulled all our credit reports to approve mortgage loans. We were paying him about $50 for a full, verified report.

We had been in business with him for about 6 months and developed a friendship. He seemed smart and was building his business.

One day, he approached me and said he was having trouble with growing and running his business. He needed an infusion of cash because he was going broke with his business model. Since we were paying him for business, it seemed like possibly an excellent investment to cut our overhead if we could get our product cheaper. He wanted to borrow $20,000.

I told him to write up a proposal on what he would do with the money on a projected P&L and Balance sheet for the next year showing how he would pay back the loan.

When he came with the projections, I was blown away. He listed his expenses as #1 His personal salary of about $5000 a month, keep in mind this guy was BROKE. #2 At the end of every month he'd spent all the revenue on business expenses and the bottom of every balance was a big ZERO. No money left over.

As I scanned all the expenses he had projected, I was shocked to find that there was no repayment for our loan to him...no payments, no payoff, nothing. He had literally given himself a healthy raise, bleeding out the money we were going to give him with ZERO plans to pay us back.

If you're going to borrow money from someone, one must show how that money is going to be repaid. It was obvious he was more interested in enriching himself on his salary. I called him up and said; "You know, there's just one problem with this. You don't show anywhere how you plan on paying our loan back. That should have been your priority to pay us back first, not give yourself a raise. Loan denied.

Lesson: Never indulge people who treat you as a secondary after thought. When someone shows you who they are, believe them. No second chances.

We kept our business with him, but eventually he had more financial problems, which forced us to move to a more stable service. Long term, he didn't survive, so it ended up being a wise decision.

Leadership Lessons:

- Recognize When Business Models Fail and Change Them Early
- Built Sustainable Models
- Control Your Burn Rate
- Cash Is King
- Eat Your Own Lunch
- Take Care of Your Investors

9

The Deepest Cut - Et tu, Brute?

My best friend of 22 years and business partner for 13 years walked into my office one day and handed me his office keys. "I quit," he said. "I've sabotaged Silverstreak Express, so you won't make payroll in 4 days. It will pull all the companies into bankruptcy absolving me of my half of the debt." And then he left. I had 4 days to save our little empire of companies.

The Ultimate Test

My best friend and I met in Jr. High School in an Art Class. We would later become roommates and start Silverstreak Express together and several other businesses over the years.

After 22 years, working side by side, I trusted him explicitly. Even more so, I truly loved him as a brother and friend. I trusted no person more with my life, our business, and money. I used to joke that we were such a ride and die team that if he ever called me telling me he had a body in his living room, I might help him bury it and go to jail with him.

It was a joke, but there might have been a bit of truth to the depth of loyalty I felt. For a long time, I'd thought we were the greatest team...to me, we seemed inseparable. I thought our team was the principal key to the success that we'd built.

I was the CEO of all our companies and the main visionary, but as Vice

President he was good at doing the routine boring repetitive tasks every business requires. In my mind, it was great. We each excelled at our strengths and could support each other's weaknesses. I would tell people who wanted to form a partnership to find this balance.

Two visionaries will just argue over who is right, and two redundant managers won't have a visionary to lead them. You need both.

A year before he finally quit permanently, we had a bunch of employees in our telemarketing department that he was in charge of, group up and quit one night. What had happened was one poisonous employee turned everyone against the company and encouraged a walkout. We never found out why.

In business or the military, this type of person is a virus and they will not only be a poor employee, they will poison the other employees and damage your company. Weed them out quickly because they are toxic.

I had gotten a call from our telemarketing manager that nine employees had quit and were making a show of doing it together and walking out with their little virus leader.

I called my partner up and was briefing him on what had occurred and trying to understand what caused this to happen. After all, this was his department and employees.

Almost immediately, he communicated to me he wanted to quit. It took me by complete surprise and shock. He said he was sick of being an entrepreneur, sick of dealing with all the hassle, and just wanted to quit.

I was stunned because it had come out of left field. I was afraid of losing my long-time partner and really didn't think I could run the business without his help. He ran one of our three core companies and the whole telemarketing 50 seat dialer division.

The Country Club Rule

I felt like Howard Stern when Jackie Martling quit. I thought my success was attached to our team and without him, I would fail. So I talked him back off the ledge for almost 2 hours and promised we would make some changes to make him feel better about staying on.

This was the biggest mistake and the dumbest decision I ever made in business. EVER. I should have let him quit. And I knew that. As I hung up, it hit me the rule that we had developed and established for employees that quit.

The one thing we had learned over all the business years was that when an employee quit, let them stay gone. For years we had employees that had quit our company come back a few weeks later wanting their job back, saying they made a mistake.

Initially, we would take them back. Then we found that usually people who are unhappy and looking to quit are not smart enough to know what they have and are constantly looking for greener pastures.

So we had to create a policy rule that I called the "Country Club Rule." Basically it said that if you quit, you could not come back for an entire year. We put this in our initial contracts so that employees would preemptively know they couldn't use us as a revolving door, and we wouldn't tolerate them coming and going.

Not only did this policy make employees think harder about quitting and chasing fairy tale promises other competitors were using to lure them away, but it would increase our retention rates and lower turnover.

There is a high cost to turnover on replacing people and the more that you can do to keep them, the better. BUT when someone quits, it's over from that moment on. Let them go, even if they come back the next day.

I remembered as soon as I hung up the phone...it came to me..."the rule is you have to stay quit." I should have just let him quit. The more I thought about it, I wondered, well let's see how he feels in the morning and maybe I should push him that way.

He came in the morning and seemed back to normal and committed to our business. I had hoped that maybe the rule didn't apply to business partners, but it did.

Here's a tip. In business, relationships etc., when someone says outright they will quit, they have just exposed the tip of the iceberg that has been cooking in their head for a long time. This is a lead up to a practiced moment where they finally express verbally what they have been thinking in their head for a long time. THIS IS PRACTICE TEST RUN SO SEE IF IT'S LIBERATING TO THEM and encouraging other ideas they have to move away and on. It's only a short amount of time till they run more test quits and then finally do.

Never Let Unresolved Issues Slide

But back to work he went and so did I. The next year was filled with trials and tribulations, mainly because he'd given up being a supportive partner, and we had major business struggles. During this time, I was struggling to change our company business models, innovate or cash bleed outs, and I was taking all the work home, carrying the load myself.

I would send him home with a notepad to come up with ideas about why we were losing money in different departments of our business…he came back with zero ideas, not seeming to care.

I would encourage him to come up with at least one idea, and he couldn't even do that. I tell this story to make people realize that when your partnerships come to this stage, it's time to end them before they end you.

A deal came up through a friend and we tried investing in a mall store to take it over and nationally franchise it. It was a hip hop store selling Sean John, Rocawear & State Property hip-hop fashion lines. After a few months of opening the store, we found we had a terrible partner.

This new partner had deceived us… it turned out his wife, who was living in San Francisco, controlled the purchasing and inventory. So after opening a mall store that was very successful and preparing to franchise it, we had to kill the deal.

The fallout was rough, and I felt alone. I had usually been the visionary, the creator, the Rambo you dropped into the jungle to clear a path for the business village to set up. But tension arose in our relationship and this wouldn't have been the first time I'd carried him through the jungle of our business life.

He had followed me like a puppy dog everywhere. "Whatever you want to do Chris" was always the answer when I'd poll him for advice.

In one exchange, he had mentioned how much our fleet insurance was, and I was stunned. I remembered asking him about the cost of car insurance for Silverstreak Express. He got angry when I told him the valuations were too high. I had asked him if he had shopped the price around on the internet.

He bristled and I could tell he was not happy and this might be a bad time to press the issue.

I had other things to run, and Silverstreak was his bag. I gave him some space as we were both smarting from wasting time on the mall franchise project. We had gotten double our money back, so the loss was more to our ego than money.

The Knife Slides In

Then it came with no warning, although you could feel the tension when he would come into the office. On a Tuesday, he walked into my office, handed me the keys to everything, and said he was quitting again. I was half stunned, but knew after the last time I needed to accept it and let him go. I was half prepared for this, but not the next bomb he had to deliver.

He told me that to ease himself from his half of the debt of the company; he had been sabotaging Silverstreak Express, the company I entrusted him to run, every day for the last year.

Therefore, we would not make payroll at the end of the week, which was four days away on Friday. It would bankrupt all three of our core businesses. The exchange was brief and over in minutes.

He seemed to think he could just get a new job at his current salary level, thinking foolishly that someone would hire him with what little real corporate experience he had. I went into survival mode with what he had just told me.

Immediately I had to find out what was going on, what he had sabotaged, and I had only four days to make payroll or bust. After he left, I sat down to see what he had done and understand it.

He had put a pile of mail out for the mailman and in the wisest move I may have ever made; I grabbed the mail back so I could see what bills were going out and what was happening.

It surprised me with the amount of payments he had sent out to various vendors. I recognized some of them because I had set them up 10 years earlier...namely, our auto insurance agency for our fleet of vehicles.

I sat there in shock for an hour or two, forcing myself to work to get through the process. I called the employees to let them know I was taking over Silverstreak Express and to report to me. Then I started going over the books to see how much cash we had, how much cash flow we had and why we would not make payroll at the end of the week. He was right.

Silverstreak was broke, but I still didn't know why it would not make payroll. I spoke with my head courier and he told me that my now ex-partner had been acting weird for sometime, blowing off customers, not changing pricing, not working on adjustments our customers wanted to make, basically driving customers away. I was reeling.

I knew I had two paths. One, accept the fate he'd delivered to me and my employees, or try to pull off the greatest comeback ever in four ticking days with a bankruptcy gun against my head. I remember looking over at the 10-year-old letter I kept on my desk from the Department Of Public Service mocking our application for Silverstreak Express.

I steeled my resolve to not be beaten; I gritted my teeth and thought: "Not today. Not this week. This is not how I'm going down."

I made a commitment to myself to do everything in my power to make payroll and save the companies or exhaust everything in the attempt. I would not go down without pulling out all the stops. It was the biggest challenge I had ever had so far in my whole entrepreneurial career.

Everything I had learned about thinking out of the box and innovating on the fly was facing the ultimate test with a four-day window.

I could have crumbled and beat myself up for the mistake I had made a year earlier by not letting him quit. Self pity could have wallowed me up, but there wasn't time. I went into "Survival Mode". Sometimes that is enough to fight another day after they have beaten you down. The fight isn't over till you quit.

These moments that seem big at the time stretch our character and later
the events seem small in hindsight because we grew. They prepare you for
the biggest fights of your life and mine was on deck staring me straight in
the face to destroy everything I'd built over 13 years with my blood, sweat
and tears.

Stopping The Bleeding

Imagine the feeling of betrayal, my best friend whom I had loved and trusted
more than anyone had dealt me the ultimate blow...one he was sure I would
never recover from. I didn't have time to consider the pain and loss, I just
focused on the fight.

I dropped everything and spent the next two days figuring out where we
were and what had happened. I literally stayed up for nearly 48 hours straight,
poring over the books, accounts receivables, everything. We didn't even have
enough in our other companies to cover the payroll.

Then I found out that many of the early vendors I had initially set up with
our business had gotten very chummy with my partner. He was treating
them as friends and not vendors. I noticed he'd sent out several payments...
it was his last payoff to his friends while he backstabbed me as his oldest and
most loyal friend.

In the last mail batch I had grabbed was several thousand dollars to his
vendor friends. For any business, if we really would not make payroll, any
smart entrepreneur would have gone late with the vendors to keep the
business afloat. We'd done that in our early years, asking vendors to carry us
60-90 days.

First stop was the banks to remove his name from the accounts. Thankfully,
I was the CEO, and it was easy to do. Then I started looking over the bills
and payments. I looked at what our fleet insurance was costing us...$5000 a
year, PER FLEET CAR.

I quickly checked pricing on the Internet by pulling up some vendors
for commercial fleet vehicles and was shocked to find out that I could get

insurance for about $1200-1600 a year instead of $5000 per year - PER CAR.

We were being ripped off at a massive over price, and these "friend" vendors he'd cozied up to and trusted had bled us out for years.

The same thing with our car repair garage. The repair had been taking our cash and making our cars last in line to repair with massive overcharges. One car had been sitting at the shop for months over a transmission.

The repair shop was so cozy with my partner they were getting away with murder. In the courier business, if you can't use your cars, and you lose money hiring rental trucks to carry the loads. So you're paying double for cars.

Over the next 48 hours, I poured over the books, trying to squeeze out every dime I could to make payroll...I stopped the checks going out, but even if they had gone out, I would have canceled them, anyway.

In a Herculean 48 hour push, I talked to employees, poured over balance sheets & P&Ls, and back accounts, trying to figure out how to save the company. There were no outstanding checks to cancel.

I changed our insurance and fired off a legal letter canceling our policy and informing them they had been ripping us off for years. I told them they needed to contact me to make a claw back settlement before I sued them.

One of the next biggest costs was our Workman's Comp payments for the State. I found the payment my partner had just made in the mail. As a standalone courier company, the percentage we paid on payroll was massive, but if they worked inside of my mortgage company, they kept a substantially much lower cost.

I acquired our courier company under our mortgage company, so it would not be a standalone business and moved the employees under the mortgage umbrella. I'd saved about $40,000 a year by this move alone.

I made calls to the vendors who had NOT been ripping us off. I explained the situation and called in the note on the power of my word and character they had known for 13 years. "I need 90 days' billing to float on payments."

They gave it to me. It was excessive to ask it, but I didn't know what other hidden bombs awaited me that my ex-partner had sabotaged.

You can see, the topics I talk about in this book are so important. In these seminal moments, everything you have built with people, character and reputation will be your only card and that will ride on everything.

Sometimes that is all you will have and you better have filled up that character bank because you will need it.

Then I sat down with what we were charging customers and tried to shore up what we were doing. I had considered raising prices, but it would shock our customers and make them quit our service. I needed every dollar. I had to leave that rail alone and not disrupt the income.

One bullet I had to bite was whether to tell my employees we were in trouble and might default at the end of the week. But thinking about it made me think of a better way. I called my oldest and closest companies that had outstanding bills and explained there had been a change of management because my former partner had embezzled some funds…they were dealing with me now again, the original person they had trusted, who had sold them nearly 13 years before.

Many expressed joy, as my now ex-partner had become a negative person to deal with. I asked if we could come pickup the checks they were sending rather than mail them. Again, I could withdraw from the bank of character I had built up for 13 years. Thankfully, we were a courier service, so picking up checks was up our alley.

Overall, we still had to borrow some money from my mortgage company to make the payroll. With nearly all the financial bleeding patched and nearly $100,000 of waste saved, the inevitable bankruptcy and bringing down of all the companies were defused. I had saved the companies, made payroll and pulled us back from the brink of bankruptcy.

My employees had always known the type of person I was, and we kept on trucking. I had saved our first company and all of our other companies from bankruptcy and his sabotage to drive us under.

The saddest part of this was how shortsighted and narrow minded my former friend and partner had become. He could have played a better card a year earlier. But remember, so could I, if someone quits on you let them move on.

The problem is their vision, not yours. If he had come to me and wanted to quit, I would have gladly taken over his debt, given him some walking money and everyone would have won.

I probably would have given him a monthly payout for a while just to nicely move him along. I would have been very rich for what he was paid that last year if I had kept it. In the end, it hurt me, but it was worse for him.

If You Cant Kill Me, Then Steal?

A couple of months after that, our delivery boxes started to randomly be stolen, and we couldn't figure it out. Then one day, one of our cars came up missing. He had stolen a car back from us that was in his name...he was stealing the corporation's property. After a while we realized what was happening...he admitted it was him. He felt it was still his property.

After a month of floating around, he found out that no one would hire him at his salary with his limited entrepreneur experience. He literally thought at his level there were employers willing to take him to an executive six figure position.

So failing at that, he started a competing courier company. Fortunately, our clients were very loyal to me. I had been the original one to enlist them and most people do not want to rock the boat with their service....another important investment in the bank of character and reputation.

Our customers stood by me as I made calls to shore up relationships and was honest about what had happened. Turns out they had missed working with me from back in the beginning.

In hindsight, we should have had contracts, but he had solicited our clients, and they stayed. The power of my personality and communicating with clients made all the difference. But now he was stealing things from the corporation.

A corporation works as a standalone entity. As its caretaker, I am the person who handles its care and assets in oversight. It was like he was stealing from another company.

In the end, the police wouldn't do anything since the vehicle was in his name, so the only other option to get him to stop stealing our mailboxes from us was to sue him. So I did.

What an interesting lesson that was. First, it started off in small claims court because I just wanted him to stop without incurring a massive amount of cost to use as an injunctive stop measure where the court could stop it if he continued to steal from us. He counter sued me. In the courtroom, the judge saw right through what he did.

He had started a new company and was stealing from us. The judge ripped into him in open court and read him the riot act, awarding us damages. I was stunned that a partner who has stood by my side for all these years watching all my mechanics and legal suits was completely ignorant. He admitted to spending a ton of money hiring attorneys.

He learned one thing from my toolbox; he appealed the case. Then it went to appellate court. This time the judge was more detailed on contracts and valuations etc. since he had no pro forma contracts or exit agreement, it did not bound him to return the stolen car. The car was in his name, but the judge ordered him to quit stealing our mailboxes.

The best moment came when he asked if he could speak to me directly in the court. The judge approved. Obviously perplexed, he asked me directly how I had saved the companies. He was stumped. I countered he was wasting nearly $100,000 a year on poor management and his cronies, and it was easy to fix (I fudged a little on how hard it was for a week).

I'll never forget the look on his face as it dropped in shock that all that money he'd been wasting was MY money now. He had betrayed his oldest and most loyal friend, lost an empire of well-paying business' future income that I had carried on for almost 13 years, and now reality was setting in how badly he'd messed up.

He tried to compete for the next 6 months with his courier company and could only scrape together some small accounts that didn't use us. There he was at my age, starting over, driving his own car like we had done 13 years earlier, driving 12 plus hours a day. It was sad.

As if karma couldn't get any better, even riding next to me for 13 years as my shadow and seeing my skills, he couldn't build a company and ended up shutting it down a few months later.

He took a job running some little retail shop in the backwoods of Oregon or Washington and went off the grid to this day on social media. To the best of my research, he never ever lived the high life that he had lived riding with me.

As I continued with our companies for almost another decade through the recession and everything I did in the recovery, losing his friend and business partner cost him a fortune.

Processing Loss & Redemption

As I referenced earlier, when Jackie Martling left Howard Stern, the story goes Stern was despondent and crushed. He thought losing his partner meant that he'd lost his essence and mojo. He wasn't even sure he could be funny anymore. As Stern found out, he didn't need Jackie. The magic sauce was always HIM. Stern had always been a rock star.

Losing a 22-year-old partnership and best friend meant I had to process the loss almost like a death or divorce. It was brutal and hard emotionally when I stabilized the company and finally I had time to reflect. I, like Stern, had thought I'd lost 50% of my mojo. But I soon realized as I looked back, I had always been a rock star, too.

Takeaways

After all this, over a decade later, for this book, I thought it interesting that even though we were 51-49% partners; I cared more about our companies than he did. I still have all the old original artwork, old way bills, corporate files and everything about the company...I had kept it, nourished it, and loved it like one of my children.

None of this stuff had mattered to him. Just getting a check and when times get tough, he quit.

To me, the lesson really tells you who cared more and why when he left, I was still the "guy," the proponent all this time, and he was the ride along on my coattails. I hadn't needed him ever. After he quit, I replaced him with

someone barely above minimum wage. That's how little work he had been
doing while taking a massive paycheck. A minimum wage secretary replaced
him.

Another lesson: If you take on partners, have a performance to payout
agreement . The person who works the hardest and provides the most value
should be paid the most, regardless of stock ownership.

How To Make A Virtual Board

So after my partner left, I had no one to bounce ideas and concepts off of,
no board to vote on ideas or advice on my business. I was basically alone.
The options were, of course, to hire a new partner, hire a board or hire an
attorney to advise me.

These options were very expensive and left with the debt of my partner. I
didn't want to spend the funds to do it.

Back in the day, we didn't have all the online options of Facebook groups
etc. to ask and bounce ideas off of for help; Many of my personal friends,
though, were entrepreneurs and one day trying to figure out how to get
advice for my business…it hit me.

Why not ask 4-5 of my close entrepreneur friends to act as what I termed a
"virtual board." So I called them and pitched the idea to them. I said, "Look, I
need a virtual board where I can play ideas and concepts off of and get advice
for my business, and since you are also a small business owner, you may need
the same.

So here's what I propose. We are on each other's virtual board, and I will
give you the same access to the ideas you are working on."

This worked exceptionally well and all my friends got on board. This was
really smart as many of them came from a broad range of businesses and
that variation could provide each of us with different points of views on any
topic.

It worked great. The principal thing is you have to give as much as you
get and be prepared to give time to someone else to bounce their ideas off of

you. It's all about the fairness of exchange and giving and getting value. (But) It worked excellently and people loved the story and ideas.

One of the biggest problems as an entrepreneur is loneliness, isolation, depression and feeling like you have the world on your shoulders. Having other people who understand your struggle can make all the difference.

Many times your loved ones that surround you do not know what being in the "guy" seat is like and the pressures you feel and what goes on in your head, but other owners know.

That's why this idea was so good. You can help each other and since there is a fair exchange of value, you don't have to pay anything for it.

And many times, helping someone get insight into their business and being the teacher, you're reminded of things that you may have forgotten or you need to work on with your business. You can do the same with the people you keep around you.

Leadership Lessons:

- Making A Virtual Board
- Vision
- Perseverance
- Hard Work
- Discovering Self Worth
- Test of Character
- Surviving The Loss Of a Partner and Sabotage
- Perseverance
- Willpower
- Overcoming Adversity
- Courage
- Survival

10

Digital Man - The Comeback

"The real glory is being knocked to your knees and then coming back. That's real glory. That's the essence of it."–Vince Lombardi

"Success is not final, failure is not fatal: it is the courage to continue that counts."
-Winston Churchill

Survival and Rebirth

How did I get started in social media? What made me start The Chris Voss Show & Podcast from the ashes 13 years ago?

Some people have made the comment that we were all flipping burgers before and suddenly we are social media marketers. I've had some people tell me my success on social media was solely because I got on Twitter early, etc. so let me speak to that. It's NOT.

During the recession of 2008-2009, I was struggling to keep all of my companies in business.

The recession was heavy. It was killing and destroying everyone's business. It wiped out my mortgage company that was nearly 20 years old. I had almost given up on my other companies because it was just too hard to sustain them, but I was trying to get it going again, despite the recession.

I had one friend tell me that because I had started so many companies and tried so many things to survive this recession, he wouldn't be surprised if it came out that I was an international weapons dealer.

I consulted with mortgage companies and banks, sadly one by one, the mortgage companies were failing, and even banks.

The Age of Twitter

One day I started hearing about Twitter. I noticed media news referencing Twitter as this new popular trending technology. About that time, Oprah joined Twitter, and it made a lot of news buzz and everyone seemed to talk about it.

In December 2008 I tried Twitter. Within a brief time, it baffled me. I didn't fully understand how it worked like many others. It was so new. I was sending messages, yet no one was replying. This is dumb, I thought, and quit. I left for a month or two, but the media hype just kept growing, so I tried it again.

It was frustrating because it was so different...I was forcing myself to figure it out and master it. Everyone was talking about how great it was, that it was the new frontier. I kept tinkering with it and trying to figure out why it was so interesting to people and why they were so excited about it.

People on Social media were crowing about Twitter and something in my vision was telling me I needed to figure out this hot new platform. As a CEO, I kept my ear to the ground so I could recognize successful trends.

I started tweeting experimental conversations while monitoring the patterns of what other people were doing. I tested what types of communications would get engaged and what would fail.

I did a ton of A-B testing like I had always done in business. Many people were posting quotes, so I started posting inspirational quotes. I think this was something people loved because we were deep in a dark, depressing recession.

As soon as I switched to posting these inspirational quotes, people started interacting with me. Suddenly the "lights" went on how Twitter worked...all

I had to do was educate myself, recognize its patterns and master it.

I promoted my companies by tweeting out their web page links. By doing this, my websites started getting a lot of traffic as people on Twitter clicked the links. I quickly realized that there was a "Tweet" button that I could push on Twitter to advertise my websites, and people clicked on them.

It took me about two months to finally master Twitter's setup. I was really excited when I received 7000 hits on my website. I started getting some business from it and traction. But it was still a struggle to get revenue as the recession was still ongoing, but it still gave me hope.

I started building more accounts and A-B testing what worked and didn't. I'd have different accounts testing various communication and content. Because I had always been so highly communicative as a CEO, my entire background was in sales and being very social.

I did all the newsletters for our corporations back in the day…I was the person who was always the biggest mouth. So social media was very easy… you communicate a lot…you share ideas. There was a lot of interaction with others, which resulted in building bridges of communication.

I think Twitter had about 30 to 40 employees and their systems were really imbalanced. You could see what was called the "fail whale" all the time, where their systems would go down. Their systems would also suspend people's accounts without reason for several days and you needed to know who to talk to for getting unsuspended.

What developed was a group of us who had become top dogs on Twitter and had figured out how it worked. I was in the top 1000 people on Twitter in followers just in my primary account. Then we started being an unofficial customer service group on Twitter, helping others navigate and deal with the suspensions.

People came to us with questions such as, "How do you do this and how do you do that". We also knew people on Twitter that we could refer to for customer service to get their accounts unsuspended.

Recession Business Breakthrough

With trial and error, I actually published an eBook called "How to keep from getting suspended on Twitter". People bought the book because Twitter's amount of suspensions was getting way out of hand. My ebook was a way of teaching people what things to do and not do.

Out of the blue, the CEO of a local company called me up. He said, "Hey, we've been seeing what you're doing on Twitter. It seems like you're really successful at it and seem to know what you're doing. We'd like to pay you to come to teach us how to do so as well." At first, I was taken aback. I was just having fun, doing my own business stuff. I was like, wait, someone will pay me to teach them how to do this silly stuff?

So I went and showed them how to use the techniques and traits that I had been using on Twitter. I left later that day with my very first check in hand for consulting as a social media trainer. Wow, I had a new business! That company started using my tricks for themselves and became very successful with it. I even spoke at their annual franchise conference.

Early on, I knew one important thing. I needed to build an audience. I didn't know what I was going to use that audience for or what the brand would be. All I knew was I needed to have many people listening to me and following me as a leader, no matter what I wanted to market or sell in the future. If you have an audience, you have power. But I didn't really know what I was going to do or what the future was.

This new frontier of Twitter and social media was like the wild west, and innovations and changes in it were happening daily. So I sat down and tried to figure out what brand I wanted to build.

Founding of "The Show"

There was the Chris Voss brand I had started. I knew I loved entertaining people and began doing minor radio shows on air at Blog Talk Radio and other apps. I've always been told I had a radio voice and, as some would say, a talkative, big mouth. So I figured what the heck, I'll start doing radio and video types of shows.

To further establish my new brand, I needed a name, a website. I asked myself what do I want to call my brand...there were so many specific names that I had in mind. However, all the websites under "social media" were taken.

Finally, what I settled on was brilliant...my brand would be The Chris Voss Show. It was not only specific to me, but was also a very general term because the Chris Voss show could be anything and adjust over time to whatever I wanted to talk about.

The significant thing about the Chris Voss show over the years has been that it has gone through several content changes.

In summary, in late 2008, I had discovered Twitter and its ability to grow business and share in the inspiration of others. I took some ideas from what I saw on Twitter and expanded it as large as I could.

I realized quickly that in this most desperate recession, that I had predicted on my blog years earlier, people needed uplifting now more than ever before. Few greater gifts can you give someone than the gift of possibilities and hope.

I'd always counseled employees and business people...I didn't become something for Social Media; it turns out Social Media had become me. Successful salespeople and leaders have always "engaged." Social Media just provided more expansive technology to do it with.

When the 2008 recession had wiped out my little empire of companies, I was left with what to do to rebuild them. It was time to pull out my old leadership toolbox and REINVENT MYSELF.

My concept was to create an inspiring blog and podcast on The Chris Voss Show, sharing what I'd learned over decades of being a serial entrepreneur. To give people ideas, tools, and hope in our darkest recession. To freely share lessons, I had spent a business fortune learning the hard old-fashioned way.

I asked myself, when I was starting out, what would I have wanted to know. What were the secrets I'd found? When hundreds of thousands of dollars were lost in profits on markets or mistakes, how did I keep my head about myself as an entrepreneur for others to learn?

The Results

My blog now comprises over 4100 posts, with about 4000 videos on YouTube, and nearly 1000 podcast episodes I've shared. I also kept a steady stream of inspiring quotes on Twitter as a complement because entrepreneurs needed the feeding of positive thoughts and ideals.

Over the last 12 years, the comments have continually encouraged me and inspiring stories I've collected of people thanking me for helping them or touching their lives. I've had people tell me on some gloomy days, they thought of ending it all. But somehow a random quote that I had put out turned on a positive light.

People who had been out of work during those first few years in the recession told me that my Twitter stream had kept them mentally and emotionally afloat. Others found my published work had made all the difference in improving the quality of their lives and turned their life on a better path.

Social Media people who've been wise enough to build strategic relationships with me grew and became successful heeding my advice.

I'm often told that people check in everyday so I can put a smile on their face. It's all these comments and feedback that have helped keep me going and giving. Giving is what I enjoy most about Social Media and with its technology I've evidenced touching changes in people's lives. We are all human beings. We should give each other hope to live

As I built the "Chris Voss" reputation and brand, "The Chris Voss Show" gathered over 400,000 followers on my social media accounts. Lots of awards flooded in. I shared a magazine cover with Steve Jobs.

For two years in Forbes magazine,I was awarded as being in the Top 50 social media rock stars based on my social media following and engagement.

When I launched The Chris Voss Show site & the Podcast in 2009, I knew I needed to build an audience. I just didn't know what to do in the long run. But I knew I needed to be interesting, charismatic, funny and, hopefully, people would like me.

Leadership Lessons:

- Survival/Rebirth
- Perseverance
- Vision
- Innovating
- Pattern Recognition
- Testing Trial & Error
- Change Your Models
- Find & Do What You Love

III

Part Three

My Top 5 Beacons Of Leadership
1. Passion
2. Vision & Innovation
3. Integrity & Trust
4. Communication & Selling
5. Character

11

Passion

The most powerful weapon on earth is the human soul on fire.
  -Field Marshal Ferdinand Foch

The Power of Passion in Leadership

In listing the Top 5 Inspiring Leadership traits in a hierarchy of importance, from my view and experience, Passion is the #1 trait a visionary leader must possess. In the end, being a visionary is the selling of ideas and getting people to embrace them. People buy products and ideas based on the movement of their hearts and minds.

Passion is one of the greatest things we have to drive human nature to or through any triumphs or out of adversity. If you have passion and operate with it as a powerful part of your personality, that shared passion can inspire others to do likewise.

An inspired leader can fire up passion when needed to convey the vision that they want to motivate their followers to get. You not only have to inspire but also MOTIVATE people with that passion.

Being a leader means you must be able to engage people emotionally to want to follow your visions and goals, and then to keep following them as part of their mantra to fight for your cause, your organization's cause and their own success.

People who exemplify genuine leadership qualities share, communicate, and instill the feeling of their own passion. Which will inspire others to WANT to buy into helping the leader achieve those same goals for the enrichment of the team and themselves as an individual.

Think of the people in history who have inspired us to do amazing things that seemed impossible. Kennedy's "Moonshot" speech, Martin Luther King's "I have a dream" speech, Lincoln's Gettysburg Address, the list goes on and on. History remembers these passionate visionaries over hundreds of years of history.

They are celebrated because they had the power to inspire and deliver their message in a way that impassioned people to go to the next level. These leaders were like a magnet, drawing masses of people by the power of their passion and personality.

These titans inspired us to dream big dreams and think that anything was possible. Imagine having that power to change the world or at least your company, your family or your life. It can happen. All it takes is developing your abilities to find your passion and then share it.

The Passionate Personality

Think of your work and leadership principles as a crafted personality. To lead, you need a passionate personality to put power behind your voice and presence. Customers, vendors, board members, employees all feel that come through when you communicate. This helps energize them and motivate people. It helps people have faith in you and builds trust.

How to Develop Passion In Your Leadership Personality.

Finding your purpose, your mission in life, identifying what you love can reveal your passion. When we talk about what we are passionate about, listen to how you communicate with more energy and drive. Find your passion and wield it as power.

Find industries you can be passionate about. Steve Jobs' dad was a fine carpenter and taught him the value of quality in making a finished product he was proud of. Steve translated that care into his work at Apple.

CEOs and entrepreneurs are passionate about their business and the love, care and creativity that they put into it, it's their baby, their creation. They gave it birth, fed it, groomed it, raised it, and protected it...for most people it's almost a living thing.

Leaders who are dedicated realize that there will be trials and tribulations, difficulties, and challenges that they will have to overcome and it's their passion that will lead them to triumph.

Learn and practice to deliver passion in your communication. When you speak, are people excited, moved, motivated? Can you light up a room of people and get them fired up about your ideas or vision? Listen and test yourself with practice to get better. Monitor how you affect people around you when you are trying to motivate or sell your vision.

How I Approach It

For me, genuinely caring about other people and their interests is something that motivates my passion. I find people interesting to me with their different paths they've taken in life. I try to understand and help them achieve their best results. Helping others and raising them up helps you. I know that a rising tide lifts all boats so lifting others will lift me.

If you genuinely care about people, their interests, when you lead with passion, they can tell. It will ooze out of your pores and they can feel it. People want to work with or for someone who has their best interests at heart who fights with and for them.

That caring is part of my core. Having that emotional connection drives me to motivate and inspire them to bigger goals.

As a leader, I feel I want to make people successful first because if I do that, then I win as well. This was very true in the days that I ran sales floors and salespeople. The more sales and commission I could inspire them to make, naturally, the more I would make.

Getting a workforce to produce is paramount in a business and leading with the carrot of motivation achieves far better results than managing with the fear of a stick. People don't perform at their best in a state of fear and being uninspired.

In the end, passion is a power that is important to wield, albeit responsibly. You also have to have logic to be a smart leader and guide your people, you can't just operate on passion and emotions, but it is so important to have it inside yourself for others as that beacon for everyone to see and catch fire from.

12

Vision and Innovation

"Don't see limits. Create bigger visions beyond your preconceived narrow limitations. Then channel all of your energy to make it a reality!" - Chris Voss

For me, "Vision" is the **2nd** most important beacon trait of a genuine leader. A true visionary is an innovator and he can see "outside of the box." He can see the future, or at least what he thinks is the future. He's Steve Jobs, Elon Musk, Jeff Bezos and others of the world who see the world as it could be, not as it is.

Again they are the "moonshot" people. Steve Job once said, "We're here to put a dent in the universe. Otherwise why else even be here?"

Elon Musk has done likewise with the Mars goal. Many of the top "space" companies have been trying new ways to do space travel. Leaders see the values and assets of their company and how they can shape innovative ideas to launch it further into the future. A skilled leader who is actively searching the distant horizons for the latest and newest thing is paramount.

Pattern Recognition and Intuition

How does one develop visionary eyesight and see into the future? Much of it comes from looking at patterns and trends, having an open mind to possibility, and keeping yourself surrounded by visionary people. This also includes looking at the world around you, educating yourself, and spitballing ideas among other smart thinkers.

Top leaders associate with other top leaders at events like Davos, Allen & Company Sun Valley Conference. They go to hobnob and network with like minds, thinking about the future of everything. Keeping smart, forward thinking people in your network is incredibly valuable.

Successful CEOs and Serial Entrepreneurs have or develop a "tuning" of pattern recognition and intuition that you learn to trust. It's a weird little voice coupled with a peaceful feeling of knowing the way ahead down the path.

Sometimes it goes against accepted assumptive logic. Sometimes, being a visionary, your board may wonder, "Okay, crazy leader, hope you're right." But that's why they have you as a CEO.

The ability to generate vision is being able to establish pattern recognition based upon how the company or markets are moving and trying to innovate to bring the company into the future with new business ideas and designs.

Being able to connect the dots on where the past meets the present can tell you where the future headed. You can then see obstacles and develop strategies on how to avoid or overcome them. Sometimes an obstacle is the future. Breaking down old paradigms or walls, disrupting, as they like to say in Silicon Valley.

By addressing pain points or seeing something from another angle and asking "what if" can open your eyes. Many industries operate as old world type thinking. Take, for instance, Uber. They disrupted the almost ancient thinking of the taxi industry model and changed the world.

Disruption

Another visionary tool is to look at things from the aperture of needing to implement change. This is something Silicon Valley constantly looks at... how can a model be completely turned upside-down? This is a great way for a CEO or entrepreneur to create new business and additional income streams.

Imagine taking a business model and looking at its limitations, then imagine completely blowing up the model and reassembling the pieces in a new way.

Disruption, a term you hear a lot in Silicon Valley, and technology innovations of "disruption models" is a very interesting way of thinking in order to re-see things in a completely new light. Instead of tweaking, adjusting, tightening, eliminating over steps or redundancy in systems, you completely look at turning the model on its head.

Sometimes you can be stuck with what was once your great business creation that is suddenly on life support and bleeding out your business. Sometimes you may have a great product or service, but you must constantly improve it before your competitors do and beat you to new innovations and markets.

Hence where the saying, "eat your own lunch before someone else does" comes from. Sometimes, to redesign your business, you may have to cannibalize your own processes in order to move into new markets or revenue streams.

Eat Your Own Lunch

A good example of this was Apple's innovation of the iPad. Apple was living off of Mac computers and its new minted iPhone sales. Steve Jobs took a crack at the tablet market even though companies like Microsoft had already brought it to market but could not get traction. With the touch screen technology of Apple iPhones, Steve Jobs knew he just had to make a larger version of his wildly successful phones.

The challenge they faced in completing it was that it was a product that could hurt their Mac Computer sales and could disrupt their own computer revenue stream.

There lies the dilemma, could the iPad be successful enough to make up for them cannibalizing their own computer sales, hoping iPads would take off and become an even larger revenue stream for the part of Apple's market it would kill?

The bet they had made on iPhones had to replace the Mac sales eclipsing far beyond their revenues from Mac sales that turned it into a whole new expansion and opportunities for their company.

The aspect they faced is if they did not force innovation on themselves and "eat their own lunch" a competitor company would likely beat them to the punch and take away their chance to be first to market.

If their competitor beat them to the market, they not only would lose the chance to have an early foothold and dominance of the emerging market, the competitor would disrupt their own sales and "eat their lunch."

How To Innovate - Thinking Outside of The Box.

A toolbox secret is how I poll, ponder, turnover, and chew on data and information. Behavior creates trends, trends create money. I'm always polling, testing ideas and concepts, A-B testing as well. I'll build social graphs and audiences, using them sometimes as focus groups.

When you are innovating for your business, trying to design new models, flows and systems to lower costs, improve profits, it can be a challenge as you are constantly designing and redesigning these systems.

Therefore, you've got to think outside of the box, especially when you are trying to upgrade a system you already created.

Since you may have created them as an entrepreneur, you're more susceptible to not being able to redesign them to be further improved. Since you built the model, you cannot see outside of the box. This is the challenge.

Re-innovating systems, processes or company factors that you built can make a challenge that creates for many a dilemma that makes it hard to improve upon your creation that once was perfect in your mind.

"There's Always a Better Way To Do Anything"

This was a belief system that I always took to heart when I was trying to innovate something new. I would tell my crew what we were trying to change or improve. And I would remind us all that there is always a better way to improve anything.

That which is made better can still be improved upon and then even more. It was one axiom I was always repeating when I was trying to improve something.

There's always a better way to do anything. Much like Moore's Law, you need to keep improving and innovating faster, quicker, and more efficiently. Being an entrepreneur means that you always have to be constantly improving your company internally.

No matter how proud you are of the innovations or cost savings you make, everything changes over time and quickly, so you have to learn to keep improving to the next level.

Being an innovator is a key skill you want to learn to do. Constantly questioning reality and your systems. How many steps are in your process for your service or product? Are there too many steps in the buying process driving away buyers? Is there a way to streamline a process to have it cost less to produce or deliver?

Sometimes it's the product/service itself, or sometimes it's the marketing. Through the business production cycle, all facets of your business can be improved constantly . Once you think from this paradigm, your mind (and your staff's) will see innovation and open your mind to think outside the box.

This is a muscle you want to develop. One challenge is that after you have improved something, it is hard to throw out that baby and make something better. It has a personal touch and love since you created it, but you must get outside of your own box to see and design it in a new light.

One of the biggest challenges we all face is when you create an internal processing system or aspect of your business, there is a complicity of assurance you get from, "okay I did that and it works great." There's a sense of pride and accomplishment.

Unfortunately, the forces of business, change, and environment can change. Programs or processes that were profitable can turn into money losers as the dynamics of business competition and markets change.

Do The Crazy Ivan

Years ago I remember seeing the Movie: The Hunt for Red October. One of
the Russian submarine captains loved to do what he called a "Crazy Ivan." A
Crazy Ivan was basically an almost paranoid operation that they would do
at regular times with an about face of the ship to see if anyone was silently
stalking behind them in another submarine.

It would be a tool I'd used to teach my staff in meetings to help flush out
all the questions or consequences of how and why we did things and how
they can be made better.

So many employees or managers will come into a business, be given the
"here's the way we've always done it, so I've never questioned why." process
and won't think twice about it ever again...just repeating the duty they were
given.

So the thing I would always challenge myself with is a Crazy Ivan to see
outside of my box. It's where you turn around and look at everything you've
done and challenge it, saying, "why do we do this and how can we do it
better."

See Your Company From The Outside

One key trick I found was to get outside of my business so I could get
perspective and think of new ways to improve my company. Many executives
take yearly or more frequent vacations to get away from their business, but
many times they fill it with family, fun, and a total break from business.

A lot of companies hire "retreats" for executives to get away so they can
clear their minds and possibly think outside the box. While many of these
provide reasonable challenges to expand the minds of people, many times
they have full schedules and activities.

I've found that to analyze my business or life, it helps for me to take a
road trip. Some of my most creative thinking came from road trips where
someone else was driving the car and I could sit in the passenger seat with a
yellow tablet pen in front of me.

It's a great way to be creative because the road is boring, there's no TV,
gaming console, distractions from your home or business. You're stuck in

116

the car with a yellow pad and focus on your business or its processes.

I'd usually pick a department or business aspect to reanalyze. Then I'd pick it up objectively in my mind, looking at the pieces of it taken apart. "Why do we do it this way, who made it operate this way?" Usually I'd remember, "Oh yes, I made that, but why did I make it that way and what did I miss in making it better or now that it's made how can I improve it.

Monitor Your Customers Experience

There's an old story about how a company who sold TV dinners discovered their sales were down, and they couldn't figure out why. The CEO announced at their board meeting that the food they would now be served would be their own TV dinners. The board quickly realized how bad the food was and took steps to improve quality.

One other trick I recommend is calling or ordering something anonymously from your company. You'd be surprised sometimes how bad your customer service is when you yourself get poorly handled by secretaries and are transferred around your phone system.

An anonymous order can also reveal that you may have to audit your order processing system that might need deep repair. I've laid off a couple of secretaries who handled customers rudely. So test and monitor for flaws that your customers may experience when they call your company.

Trust me, your customers will often leave your business without telling you. Unfortunately, 96% of unhappy customers don't complain, however, 91% of those will simply leave and never come back. It's probably better if you listen to complaints or test your own.

Not to mention, a dissatisfied customer tells between 9-15 people about their experience. And around 13% of dissatisfied customers tell over 20 people according to the White House Office of Consumer Affairs.

The Power of Asking Questions

Years ago, I learned from Anthony Robbins that ASKING QUESTIONS are a huge part of finding answers you need. Our subconscious minds are constantly working and coming up with many ideas to help us accomplish what we need.

Asking questions is a great way to help yourself or the team come up with answers that challenge the status quo.

Many times, you may have to look at not just adjusting or tweaking your systems, but basically rethinking the complete model that you have.

I used to make my close circle of friends and employees help me resolve challenges for the business or ways to improve it. I'd give people yellow legal pads and say, "Here's a yellow pad to write your ideas about anything you can think of on it. Even in this digital age, I like the concept of a hard yellow pad with lines.

It gives you something concrete you have to face. You could download some Note mobile app, but a plain yellow pad is not bashing you with notifications, so you can focus on the empty page in front of you. The multiple lines also demand that you come up with many ideas. It calls you and demands you to fill it out.

At first, this can intimidate, but once you embrace it…it's like an art piece that easily helps to cue the pump and get the creative juices flowing. Often you just need to break the ice and write something down. Starting by just jotting an idea down is the hardest part to get it started, but usually once you get going, you'll have a full page.

Sometimes I call it spitballing where we throw out ideas, no matter how crazy or unreal. Just write them down, think of visions and possibilities, don't burden them with having to think about how to make them happen, just use the notepads to flush out ideas. Not all ideas will be winners, but some can develop or merge into other ideas.

Sometimes you can write just a fraction of an idea or something off the wall, bring it back to the group and compile it…then have everyone share the ideas they wrote in their notepads. Hopefully, out of all that, serendipity will happen, resulting in a merging of innovative ideas.

13

Honesty, Integrity & Trust

The supreme quality for leadership is unquestionably integrity. Without it, no real success is possible, no matter whether it is on a section gang, a football field, in an army, or in an office.
  -Dwight D. Eisenhower

One of the most important beacons one sends forth is the character traits of integrity, honesty, and trust. For the **3rd** top trait, the building of a leader is paramount to have these three elements to have a leadership style character.

Merriam-Webster defines these 3 qualities as:

1. Honesty: adherence to the facts and fairness and straightforwardness of conduct
2. Integrity: the quality of being honest
3. Trust: assured reliance on the character, ability, strength, or truth of someone or something

Each one builds upon the other and if the people you are trying to lead find you lacking in any of these, there can be a complete breakdown of their interest in following you. It's important for you to be self-aware of these standards and how you espouse them that is conveyed to your people.

We could write an entire book on this topic, but let's move forward with some examples of applying and building upon these 3 items.

Authenticity & Transparency

What does being Authentic mean to you and how is it applied to leadership? How would you define it? According to the dictionary: Authenticity is the quality of being genuine. Authenticity builds honesty, integrity and trust based on your words and actions.

Authenticity to me presents itself in several factors: trust, transparency, compassion, empathy, lifting, etc. Being authentic means speaking and living your truth in such a transparent way that others can see and measure. People have to see and feel that you live your life to your core values or that of the company.

Sit down and make a list of your core values that are most important to you personally or to your company. Then put them in order of most important to you from 1 to 5, one of course being the most important. This can give you a structure that you can use to understand what is important to you, what makes you tick, and also what values you want others to see in you.

One myth many people have is that their leader must always exhibit perfection and success, but many times, the aspect of an outstanding leader is allowing people to see his/her own personal failures and as well as how he/she responds to it and recovers from it.

A fallen leader's comeback story is always inspiring. Showing people you can fail and succeed is a hallmark of a leader.

One way leaders build trust is through authenticity and transparency. Not only being true to oneself but true and open to others, letting them see not only your leadership skills but your humanity.

You can be a leader who thinks you don't have to telegraph your style or how you operate to the value you espouse to others in your company...but you need to realize we telegraph that communication visually through our words and actions.

One thing I learned with having big audiences is they are always listening

120

and keeping notes on your authenticity and if you are really living your truth. They're tracking. I think one mistake people make is they don't realize that there is a stack of impressions people are taking from that communication.

Part of it means speaking your truth and being truthful, even though some experiences you may not want to share. Let me talk to you about how this works - many times, sharing our pain or struggle helps others and will bind them to us with trust and resolve, knowing that we overcame loss.

It's hard sometimes to be open and authentic. But many times, as a leader, showing how we handle pain and trials can help others respond to the same.

Years ago, Shadow, my oldest "first child Husky" who had been suffering from seizures for years, had a massive seizure for a half an hour and wouldn't come out of it. I rushed her to the emergency room, and they told me her temperature had been off the chart and likely had destroyed any brain function she had, and the only way to stop the seizure was to release her from it all. So I had to let her go.

In one hour, my life of almost 14 years with my first child dog was over. I came home an emotional wreck. No one close to me had died in 27 years. I had no previous to draw from...I was wide open emotionally. As I sat there, downing vodka, hoping I'd never wake again, I poured my heart out on a Facebook social media post.

I let it all bleed out as painful as it was...my crushing loss laid raw for all to see.. I remember grappling for the longest time about sharing it; it was so open and painful, but to hide my pain and sorrow would not have been authentic.

I struggled to hit the post button. I didn't want to share my pain and raw feelings. My heart felt broken as though it could never heal, yet it was embarrassing as a man to emotionally expose the deep hurt and sorrow I was suffering. After grappling with it for a while, the effect of the vodka made it easier to press "post."

I remember right after I panicked, thinking, what have I done? I've completely opened myself up and shared it. I reopened the file and thought about taking the emotional stuff out or just all out deleting it.

Drained, I left it in case I didn't wake up in the morning. It would be my final work. The next morning, calls from close friends awakened me. I remember being so angry that I was still alive as the rush of pain and reality washed over me.

What happened by bearing that level of transparency and authenticity gave me so many lessons and value. It's amazing how much I've learned. Throwing one's own pity party at first might have seemed like a selfish act, but it turned out to help so many other people. I didn't have a clue that sharing my grief would give people an emotional reference story to me as a leader.

People seeing others suffer through loss and closure did so many things:

1. I had people write to me publicly and many times privately, sharing not only their stories, but offering words of love and support with advice on how to get through it.

2. It helped many people find closure with their own losses. Seeing me in my pain, they realized they were still suffering from lack of closure on their own personal losses, saying, "I never realized I hadn't gotten closure when my dad or dog died, etc."

3. Years later, people remembered those authentic moments I shared. Especially how I handled them as a leader by helping others to know that they were not alone in their grieving process.

I learned that sharing and getting support from the community helps others more than ourselves. All the painful heartfelt stories that I shared in an act which seemed so selfish was actually a loving gift that helped so many more people in a constellation of communities to improve the quality of life in others.

It blew me away how many people it helped...an emotional bond that lasted a long time. Which Is really important in building a relationship with your audience and employees.

The Power to do what's right

Just before the 2008 great recession, some investors from China approached me to launch and build a mortgage company with them in Las Vegas.

The value of Las Vegas homes was rocketing through the roof price wise. The investors wanted to have a mortgage company, but they needed a mortgage broker with an active license that could run the operations and build it.

I thought it would be a pleasant break from running my company and let someone else handle the purse. I was still running my courier company in Utah from Vegas.

I hired mortgage loan officers quickly and spent the next 60 days building one of the fastest growing mortgage companies in Las Vegas. In fact, before our partnership collapsed, I was looking to open multiple offices across the valley. It looked great.

Early on, I started having problems with my demanding investors that were US citizens but had come over from China. I started having friction with the key investor.

First, it started with racial and sexist comments from him to a point that I had to ask him not to come into the office for the employees' protection.

In spite, he changed our original 10% commission cut of every deal. The breaking point came when he wanted to have his family's loan done with dubious references. I walked into his office one day and he asked me to sign a Verification of Income for his mother, whom I'd met…she was retired and beyond the working age.

He wanted me to do a bad loan for his family. I was aghast. I wanted nothing to do with it. As we argued, he told me he wanted to do the same fake documents for himself and the rest of his family's refinances.

It was painful as I thought of all the work I had already put into the company, but I still resigned. I had started one of the fastest growing companies in the marketplace, replicating my success years earlier. However, there was no way I could have myself affiliated with illegal loans.

Sometimes you have to take a loss to do what's ethically right. Keep your truth and dignity. It's costly, it's painful. I could go to jail for what they wanted me to do, and I could lose my license and the ability to produce mortgages.

Being powerful in integrity to yourself and others, people will see and
judge you as a leader. It can follow your reputation to the end of your days.

14

Communication and Selling

"The art of communication is the language of leadership."-James C. Humes

I rank communication as being the **4th** most important leadership skill. If you can effectively communicate your passion, your vision, and impart that to your followers, then all is lost. You could have the grandest dreams and foresight, but nothing will matter if you can sell your followers on the merits of their possibilities.

Top 5 leadership traits:
1. Passion
2. Vision
3. Trust
4.Communication
5. Character

When you combine the Top 5 leadership traits with your ability to communicate, you can sell and inspire people to move mountains for and with you. If you lack excellent communication skills, take courses and get trained.

A great communicator is always advancing his ideas, putting them out for debate, and sharing his vision for the future.

When I am selling my ideas, I watch for the emotion I fire up in them. Do they get excited, or become motivated? You want to move people and bind them to your foresight and the course to achieve it.

Always Be Communicating and Selling Everyone on The Big Vision

There are lots of influential books that focus specifically on sales, but I want to share some lessons here that are unique.

My background has always been in marketing and sales. Everything that you do as a CEO is mostly sales. You sell your employees; you sell your board; you sell your vendors; You sell your investors; you sell everybody the vision of why they should work with you.

Everything in life is sales. When it really comes down to it, you sell your partner every day on why they should stay with you and why you are the best person for them in their life. You sell your children, why they should be good. When they should do their chores, and why they should follow the rules, or at least I hope you do.

Listening Is The Biggest Part Of Communication

Listening is a skill that takes much practice. I learned this over the years while doing my podcast. This is one of the few vaunted skills that many people don't develop or excel at these days. Everyone is looking at their phones, bored with everyone.

Active listening is so important. If you really want to get to know people and learn what they are communicating...this is one of the most important things about being a leader. Listening, collecting and analyzing data is so important.

In today's world, it seems no one listens to each other. So listening is a premium. Your body language also gives away whether you are listening.

"What Are You Trying To Accomplish?"

I picked this up in the days of working at the car dealership. There was this

126

new thrust of sales techniques to get away from greeting customers with the age old question "Can I help ya?" Customers had reached a point where they had almost a subconscious brush off reaction to it.

It's a direct question with an easy deflection, especially on the car lot. "I don't need help" is the usual reply. No customer wants to think that they are helpless. It's disabling to them. Instead, we were to ask, "What are you trying to accomplish?" I took it to heart. It made it more goal centered, and I perfected the art of it.

"What are you trying to accomplish" does so many things:
1. It helps break the ice.
2. It presents to the customer that you have an interest in listening to and helping them succeed in their goals.
3. It communicates that you care and instead of being a salesperson that is focused on getting the sale, you show you are interested in helping them.
4. The actual key to this also is to focus on listening. Ask and then get out of the way. DEEPLY listen to the response. Ask questions to clarify and show you are listening and caring.

I taught my salespeople to write what the customer says in reply and then use those items to help sell your product/service to the customer. It helps eliminate a ton of problems. I perfected it with my staff and trained all my salespeople to ask their first question, "what are you trying to accomplish?"... and then listen.

If I caught a salesperson not using it, they'd get corrected. Anytime a salesperson would quit using the line, we'd have an unhappy customer event. It would always come back to not caring about the customer and listening.

Shut Up And Listen

The 2nd most important part of this process is for the salesperson to shut up and LISTEN. So many times over my career, when working with salespeople, they will commandeer or overwhelm the customers. They will try to wrestle them down with what the salespeople are trying to sell or what they PERCEIVE the customer wants.

Sometimes it's dictated by sales bonuses or contests that influence a salesperson to hustle a customer into buying something they don't want but is only in the salesperson's interests.

Many customers will resist pushy salespeople, but play along. When the final signing moment comes, they will refuse to sign in backlash. I rarely saw this in my companies, but when I did, it became clear the sales person had never asked what the customer wanted to accomplish.

In fact, many times, the customer would want a totally different service/product than the one the sales person lazily put them into by assuming.

In our mortgage business, say for instance, the client wanted a 15 year loan, but the salesperson did not ask or listen and assumed they wanted a 30 year loan.

Then at closing, the client would be angry because the loan officer had not listened, asked questions or fulfilled their needs in the end.

By asking the client up front what specific requests they have regarding the type of loan, etc., you show you put their interests FIRST and that you are listening to them. Then you can help them find the best product or service and help highlight the aspects of what you are selling to customize it for the customers' goals.

As the CEO, when I would get a call from the closing title office with a mad customer, it was always a salesperson who hadn't asked the client what they were trying to accomplish and had "slammed" the sale and the client was not happy.

Many times we would have to go back and repackage the loan. Other times, I would have to refund enough of our fees to make the client happy and get them to close.

It's so very important to understand why your consumers love your products or services. Interview them and find out how it's working for them and how they are using it. We would often find people using our products in a variety of ways that were not intended or hadn't thought about.

15

Character

"There are no failures of talent, there are only failures of character." -
Unknown

Fifth: A leader's character is everything. It is a map of his strengths and
weaknesses that he must not only use, but improve upon. The grand tapestry
of these traits is one that every leader should develop into a broad base from
which to lead from.

Yes, you can have exceptional talent, but the breadth of your character
defines you and sets the tone for your leadership style. All eyes are on you
and your character, combined with your behavior, will define your true
intent and meaning for your followers.

CULTURE

As a leader, you set the culture and management style by your BEHAVIOR.
The organization becomes you...you are the beacon that shines on all of your
employees, vendor, investors board and other people.

It's also important to be self aware of the personality you have and use.
That awareness allows you to adjust to necessary changes in order for your
company to grow exponentially.

My Leadership Traits From My Stories and Lessons:

- Attitude
- Accountable responsibility
- Analyze Your Competitors Know Their Weaknesses
- Always Be Testing, Trying, Experimenting
- Be an Entrepreneur or an "Intrapreneur"
- Believing in it with passion
- Bravery
- Built Sustainable Models
- Business Modeling
- Business Collections & Bankruptcy
- Control Your Burn Rate
- Cash Is King
- Cash Flow Is King
- Challenging and Breaking Models
- Character
- Challenge Social and Business Norms
- Courage
- Control Inexperienced Partners
- Customer Service
- Don't Price Yourself Short
- Don't ASK for the sale, ASSUME IT. CLOSE the sale.
- Discovering Self Worth
- Drive
- Eat Your Own Lunch
- Empathy
- Ethics
- Feedback, Adapt and Innovate
- Hard work
- Handling Rejection
- Innovation
- Innovating

- Kiting Cash & Contracts Can Backfire
- Knowledge
- Learning to Sell & Service Customers
- Learning from Rejection and Failure
- Learning To Think Outside The Box
- Learn From Your Darkest Moments & Grow
- Manage Your Attorneys - Understand the Process
- Making A Virtual Board
- Motivation
- Perseverance
- Pattern Recognition
- Only One Person Can Lead
- Overcoming Adversity
- Powerful Negotiation Tactics
- Paradigm shifts
- Passion
- Perspective
- Perseverance
- Performance measuring
- Preparation, practice is everything
- Rejection
- Recognize When Business Models Fail and Change Them Early
- Recognizing my weaknesses & filing them in
- Self-awareness
- Self-regulation
- Self-Reliance
- Social skills
- Speak & Live your truth.
- Scotoma (Blind Spots)
- Selling & Closing
- Survival/Rebirth
- Self Education
- Surviving The Loss Of a Partner and Sabotage

- Seek Competitive Advantages
- Testing Trial & error
- Testing & Innovating
- Test of Character
- Thinking out of the box"Where the Red Fern Grows" Raccoon Lesson - Don't Let Greed Take You To Your Death
- Vision
- Willpower
- Work Ethic
- You Can Say Almost Anything If You Smile

IV

Part Four

Leadership Toolbox & Final Thoughts

16

Leadership Toolbox

"It is not the critic who counts; not the man who points out how the strong man stumbles, or where the doer of deeds could have done them better. The credit belongs to the man who is actually in the arena, whose face is marred by dust and sweat and blood; who strives valiantly; who errs, who comes short again and again, because there is no effort without error and shortcoming; but who does actually strive to do the deeds; who knows great enthusiasms, the great devotions; who spends himself in a worthy cause; who at the best knows in the end the triumph of high achievement, and who at the worst, if he fails, at least fails while daring greatly, so that his place shall never be with those cold and timid souls who neither know victory nor defeat." - *Theodore Roosevelt*

Most successful leaders and business people have a toolbox they use, so when something in their business stops working, they can have a resource to fix it. Sometimes it's just rules to remind them to stay in their lane of operation.

So we've already covered in the book a few tools from my business "Leadership Toolbox" in the previous chapters. I'll be expanding tips for bonus content, go to BeaconsOfLeadership.com for more ongoing details.

Here are some more of my tools & lessons that I always use when I need them:

Be A Strategic General

Starting in 4th grade, I began consuming history books about generals, war and strategy. Biographies on generals like Douglas MacArthur, George Patton, Dwight D. Eisenhower. I built models of warships and read about the theaters of warfare like the Battle of Midway, etc. Strategic general games like Risk, Stratego and other online strategy games I played relentlessly into my 20s. When I analyze business or even life, this is the core of my outlook: strategy. I access the battlefield, map strategies and then engage, adjusting like a general in fluid combat. **This shapes the core of my thought process as a leader. I am a strategist.**

Go Back to Basics

Sometimes in my business when I would have a successful core model. It would be profitable, but I would be constantly tweaking it to make it more complex to expand its use. Then it would STOP working suddenly. Or sometimes I would find I had spread myself too thin, or I was trying to get fancy with too many things. Sometimes, I get too comfortable and lazy.

The tool from my toolbox that I would always remember was the line from Coach John Wooden: "GO BACK TO BASICS." I'd gotten off the track of what was making me successful and I needed to get back to the core fundamentals.

"I believe in the basics: attention to, and perfection of, tiny details that might be commonly overlooked. They may seem trivial, perhaps even laughable to those who don't understand, but they aren't. They are fundamental to your progress in basketball, business, and life. They are the difference between champions and near champions."-Coach John Wooden.

There's a story that runs around motivational speakers that Coach Wooden would tell basketball players that were spending too much time doing fancy shots, layups, half court shots, etc. They needed to get back to basics.

He'd make them work the "keys" and free throw line near the basket. Probably because he knew some of the most important game plays come out of this area.

So if you find yourself or your business off track...remind yourself to "Go back to basics." If getting fancy and complex stops working, go back to your core fundamentals. You can use this in business and life.

"The Only Stupid Question Is The Unasked Question"

I've forgotten where I picked this up from, but when I started my companies, I was mindful of what kind of environment and culture I would seed. I wanted to build a "learning organization" that I'd read about in many business books. A learning organization is one that can be agile and grow with change and adapt.

It gives a healthy environment where people can learn and the company can grow to be smarter and more innovative...not a company of paranoid people with closed off minds.

I've seen too many organizations where employees spend all day making memos to cover their behinds in order to make sure they are never blamed for anything. They are paranoid about being called out in a toxic environment.

There's a parable that has been shared around, and though it has many versions, the lesson is the same. I'll tell you the version I heard. A young couple marry and the wife cooks their first Thanksgiving turkey for her new husband. Upon the turkey being placed on the table, he finds the legs had been cut off and served separately. Shocked, he asked her why she had cooked the turkey that way.

She replied that was the way her mother had taught it to be cooked, cut the legs off and served them separately so without question she had always done so.. Curious, the husband got his wife to call up their mother-in-law to find out why she had taught the daughter to cook a turkey in this manner.

The mother replied, "This was the way I've always done it and my mother taught it to me as well." So they rang up her grandmother to find out why. The same reply came from my grandmother, "This was the way I've always done it and my mother taught it to me as well."

Now, with the mystery deepening, they decide to call up the elderly great grandmother to ask her why she had taught 4 generations of daughters to cook a turkey in such a manner. The great grandmother replied, "In the older days of stoves, there was not enough room to fit a whole turkey, so we had to cut off the legs, cooking them separately to make due.

And there it was. Four generations of people never questioned the "why" of how they did things, just mindlessly going about what they were taught. Many people do this in life and business. They sleepwalk through what they do, never questioning it.

Therefore, it is paramount to teach your employees to understand the "why" of how things are done and encourage them to question and innovate.

The worst thing I hate to hear when I ask an employee "why do you do it that way?" and he replies, "I don't know, this is the way I was taught and how we have always done it." When I hear that, it's a signal to me that a department or business process is ripe for innovation or disruption.

One of the key rules of my company's culture was the axiom, "the only stupid question is the unasked question." So let's break it down. What does that mean? Basically, it means, "There are no stupid questions here. You are in a safe zone where you will not get mocked or treated as ignorant if you ask something that you are unsure of. We want you to be comfortable learning what you don't know. Conversely, don't be stupid, people who don't ask questions are."

You want to create a culture where people can ask if they missed something in training or something communicated to them was missing or they misunderstood it...this will build their confidence.

When people don't fully understand how things work, this can cost you a fortune. There were so many times in my business where a new employee or someone appointed to management comes out of training and won't admit they didn't understand some of the key points.

It's usually the one person who will screw something up because they didn't understand, resulting in the loss of possibly thousands or tens of thousands of dollars to your small business or large.

I'd advise you to adopt this in your office and make it healthy for people to learn. Mind the environmental culture you build and you want to build that from the start.

The Own It & Control It Lesson

After hitting two home runs out of the park in our first two years, I felt empowered. I was looking for a new company to bring in additional income. But we needed a business that didn't need a workforce and could be automated. This was still in the pre-internet brick and mortar business days.

When I was younger, I was aware of 1-900 dating PHONE lines. All you needed was to buy a system number off of a 1-900 phone bank supplier, set up what type of dating app you wanted, with prompts and advertise it.

The significant thing is, if your ads work, people will spend hours a day, paying per minute, making you money 24.7. Setup, run ads and collect checks.

So the idea of having one of these money makers when they were so popular and automated seemed like the perfect third company solution. Our first company was Silverstreak Express, our second was Park Place Mortgage and to keep the theme up, this new company I called Boardwalk Entertainment.

I found someone in Chicago who was selling a used phone number line and all we had to do was buy the line and set it up with the phone bank owner. The owner of the phone bank service ran all the records, payment collection, etc.

Once bought, all we had to do was run ads and collect checks. It was weird to not be in control of the business and relying on someone else to run it, collect and pay us like almost a job, but, hey, it was a 3rd bonus line of income.

After buying and setting up the line, off we went. I had set up the classic dating 1-900 line where it was an early form of a dating app and you could call in and hear people's dating pitches and contact them. Women posted for free, men paid. It went over like gangbusters.

In the first 2 months, we had gotten our investment back, so I amped up our ads in the newspaper and other places. The money flowed in significantly.

The one thing we had just accepted as normal since we were new was that 90 day payouts were normal. Since it was credit card based, there are sometimes chargebacks, so we gave it no thought.

I kept running ads and piling up a profitable amount of money. It was my 3rd home run profitable business I'd built in just a few months AGAIN.

Around the time for us to get paid, the check had not come. We started leaving messages at the central phone bank that ran everything. Then we were called by the FCC, the Federal Communications Commission. They were calling to tell us they had seized all the central phone bank's company and all the lines were locked down, including our lines indefinitely.

Then we got the story of what had transpired. The guy who had owned the phone bank system had gone on a cocaine bender and bought two Ferraris with everyone's money. He had gotten busted by the FCC, who oversees phone lines, after defaulting on everyone, including now us.

The money was gone, and we just had to give it all up and move on. I was never informed by the FCC what was occurring in their ongoing investigation…our money was lost.

Out of that, I formed a very important lesson that I swore I would never do again. If you don't own it or control it as a majority, DON'T INVEST IN IT as a business.

It was a valuable lesson, and we learned to never do that ever again. Over all my years, I've heard of so many partnerships and businesses that my friends had gotten involved in and because they did not own majority control, they would get screwed when push came to shove in a fight over the business.

Lesson: For the small, medium-sized business owners, my rule is if I don't own it or control 51% or more, I don't do it. I'd rather invest in something I own 100%. There may be times where there are exceptions to this rule, maybe in real estate deals or other investment vehicles, but partners can be headaches when they go bad. I'd rather control my destiny.

One final thought: if you're thinking of starting a partnership with another person, consider who has the most business experience and value. It would be wiser to not offer a full partnership position up front and just HIRE the person. Later, when they prove their value, you can offer it to them as a bonus.

Lawyers working for Law firms have to prove themselves with hard work and dedication, hoping to one day be made a partner. I recommend the same. As in all partnerships, everyone is all friends and happy until the "money gets on the table" (the revenue rolls in) and that's when you find out the type of people you are in business with. Make people earn a partnership position.

If You're Not Growing, You're Dying.

This is true in life and business. If you're not expanding your mind, your muscles and working to improve yourself, you may find yourself left behind by others who do. Change is constant and life is about SURVIVAL. The same is true for your business. Every month, your revenues and assets should grow, not retreat.

Whether you are going up in revenues or down after a few months, a trend line can be assessed, and you must pay attention to it. Make sure your customer base is growing too. If you're losing more customers than adding, you have a problem. Sure, you can have a terrible month or two, but several down months can spiral into a tailspin, making it hard to recover.

Keep this tool in mind. Always be growing. If you find you're trending downward, fix it immediately. Stem the losses and bleeding "asap". Things usually get worse. Regarding the prior lesson, it might be time to get "back to basics."

Look The Dragon In The Teeth

Somehow I'd started using this saying, whether I had made it up or overheard it, I don't remember. I recall that when our mortgage company was very young; we were expanding and do more loans.

Unfortunately, we owned a really cheap copier that could not keep up with the enormous stack of papers required to file mortgage loans. We needed to buy a new expensive copier to handle it. Yet we were still tight on how we spent money and invested in the business.

Me and my business partner fretted over this large expenditure being the most we'd spent on any equipment and whether it would be worth it. So I came up with "let's look the dragon in the teeth".

I listed all of how spending the money could go wrong. We reviewed them and could determine different things we could do to mitigate any fallout and live with the results. Once we were comfortable with the risk, we bought the big copier.

Turned out shortly after that our growth exploded and we had to buy even bigger copiers, but the lesson was learned. Strategize and analyze the big decisions you make and the downsides.

If you can "look the dragon in the teeth " and live with it, it's much easier to make those decisions. The Crazy Ivan tool is also in the same tool venue as this thought process.

The 80/20 Rule

From the time I learned of the 80/20 rule in business, I had tried to beat it. Basically, the rule states that out of 100% of your customers, 20% will bring you 80% of your revenue. The same is true of employees, especially in sales. I worked hard over the years to beat this rule, but finally I just realized I need to accept it.

The important thing to do is to recognize it. You must always take extra care of the core 20% because losing them can devastate your bottom line. Make sure you're expanding your customers and employees in attrition to fill potentially new customers or employees that will be your best.

*I'll be expanding tips for bonus content, go to BeaconsOfLeadership.com for more ongoing details.

17

Final Thoughts

To laugh often and much: To win the respect of intelligent people and the affection of children, to earn the appreciation of honest critics and endure the betrayal of false friends; to appreciate beauty, to find the best in others, to leave the world a bit better whether by a healthy child, a garden patch, or a redeemed social condition; to know even one life has breathed easier because you lived. This is to have succeeded. - Ralph Waldo Emerson

I've interviewed many brilliant successful authors on The Chris Voss Show Podcast and I remember one of them telling me a great story that moved me deeply on how she motivated herself to keep writing books.

On one of her book tours, she met a woman who had been in prison. The woman told her that her book had not only inspired her, but other women inside the prison...many of them loved it. From then on, when she wrote on her computer, she kept a picture of that ex-inmate within eyesight to remind her of the reader who needed her writing the most.

As I wrote this book, I remembered how almost impossible I thought it would be for me, at age 18, to ever succeed in business. The odds of success & not conforming to social norms made the deck stacked against me and many people stood in my way. The lonely nights when I paced my office searching for innovations or resolutions. Then came failure and betrayal that was soul crushing and sometimes took every ounce of my being to get back up, like a boxer, bloody, wounded, to fight through the next round.

I know the thrill of the highs when everyone loves you and the hell of the lows where you are left all alone and no one returns your calls. The winning and the losses.

Somewhere out there, it might be you, or someone you can give this book to, that is struggling to become a leader, to succeed in business or life. That's who I mostly wrote this book for. To give you stories, lessons and tools to survive and achieve your goals.

Through all the dark times I endured, looking for the light at the end of dark tunnels…I found the way. I just kept learning the lessons and fighting. And so can you.

So I hope this book brings light and confidence to you. I hope you will use it to be the best leader you can be and inspire those around you as well as share it with others to make the world a better place. Don't let the "rules" of society, business, or dogma hold you back.

THINK OUTSIDE OF THE BOX. Don't hide your skill or talents. Embrace them.

Be the Lighthouse that shines forth a beacon of light that changes the world.

Shine on.

18

9 Dot Puzzle Solution

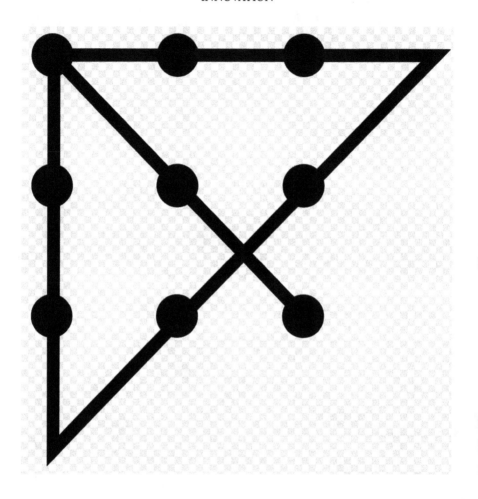

About the Author

Forbes Top 50 recognized, CEO/Host of The Chris Voss Show, Author, Consultant, Speaker, YouTuber, Coach, Many Awards, Audience over 300,000 on Social Media. 35+ Year Serial Entrepreneur.

You can connect with me on:
- http://beaconsofleadership.com
- https://twitter.com/ChrisVossShow1
- https://facebook.com/BeaconsOfLeadership
- http://thechrisvossshow.com
- https://www.facebook.com/ChrisVoss
- https://linkedin.com/in/ChrisVoss
- https://itunes.apple.com/podcast/The-Chris-Voss-Show/id343172752?

- https://instagram.com/ChrisVoss
- http://youtube.com/ChrisVoss

Subscribe to my newsletter:
- https://mailchi.mp/a226868dbb4f/1

Also by Chris Voss

Printed in the USA
CPSIA information can be obtained
at www.ICGtesting.com
LVHW011647271223
767218LV00007B/309